Bite-sized World

A memoir of travel, food and live entertainment

RUTH BADLEY

First Published 2021 by Inglebooks, Mount Bures

Copyright © Ruth Badley 2021

The moral right of the author has been asserted

ISBN: 978-1-9161195-3-6

INGLEBOOKS

Also by Ruth Badley

Memoir

Where are the grown-ups?

For Tim with love

CONTENTS

Preface

Stay at Home

Stay at home? A contrary opening to a memoir based on travel, but a familiar refrain during 2020. This book was conceived in March of that year when the stay at home imperative signalled the first, futile attempt by the UK government to control the spread of Covid-19. We were innocents back then, with no concept of how much worse it would all be by the end of that year and into the next.

As the freedom to travel disappeared in the wake of the global pandemic my memory served me well. From my armchair, recollections of recent, relatively carefree worldwide journeys nourished my need to remain hopeful. As the here and now became ever more unpredictable and uncertain, thoughts returned to the places we had been, some little more than a month before the UK population was first ordered to Stay at Home to Save Lives.

In February, 2020 Hobart had been the final stop on our first ever visit to Tasmania. With a stunning sea view we lingered over an outdoor lunch at the capital's magnificent Museum of Old and New Art (MONA). Hobart! At the time it felt a world away from a dangerous viral menace with the capacity to spread with ease across borders, oceans and continents.

It was hot that day and we shared a table in the shade with a couple on a day trip from Sydney. A low-cost flight, so easy and convenient they said. The conversation flowed and they naturally asked us where we lived. She had a brother in the UK. 'Yeah, he's a community policeman. A big Australian guy,' she told us.

We live in a village on the border of Essex and Suffolk, so tend to mention the nearest towns and cities that we think others might have heard of. 'We're between Sudbury and Colchester.'

She looked up immediately, recognition in her eyes. 'He's based in Sudbury.' It was one of those "small world" moments that made us all throw our heads back and laugh.

We've yet to come across an Australian policeman in Sudbury but if we do, we will be sure to tell him we met his sister and she gave us a great dinner recommendation. The steak we had at the city's *Ball and Chain Grill* later that night was first class. Hobart is a long way to go for an excellent steak but a global pandemic is a reminder that it is indeed a small world when it comes to contagious disease.

Tasmania was part of a five-week itinerary that also included Dubai and mainland Australia, both places where we had once lived. The coronavirus was a crisis in Wuhan before we left the UK, and during our travels news and pictures emerged showing the terrible human toll the disease was taking in northern Italy and Iran. The places affected seemed so random, the outcomes grimly surreal.

By the time we landed in Bali social media reports suggested rumours of lockdown had prompted panic buying in the UK, leading to shortages of basic items. I shrugged and resisted the impulse to order more toilet rolls than usual in the online supermarket delivery, arranged from Lombok for our return home. We had our temperatures taken several times during a stopover in Singapore and listened in sympathy as a taxi driver told us how a drastic reduction in Chinese visitors was affecting business.

As the months passed and the virus took hold in the UK, tourism, hospitality and the entertainment sectors were hit hard. Jobs that relied on a culture of eating out, going to the theatre or travelling to another country swiftly disappeared. In the absence of communal leisure, sport and culture the desire for a return to normal life intensified. The health crisis that compelled us to all to stay two metres apart from others made it impossible for those sectors to function safely and profitably.

I spent a good deal of time during 2020 feeling angry at the way this havoc was wreaked on our wonderful world. I missed the simple, uncomplicated pleasure of sharing food with family and friends, of standing in the crowd at a rock concert, of seeing the play that all the critics were raving about. I longed for the minor inconveniences of international travel and the luxury of checking for the reassuring shape of a passport in a jacket pocket for the umpteenth time.

This memoir of selected travel experiences was both a benign gesture of resistance during troubled times and a belief that a version of normality would return. The majority of the pieces originate from 2015-2017 when we had the opportunity to move to Dubai, and I blogged about aspects of our new life in the United Arab Emirates. Already a key hub for international air travel and tourism, Dubai's growth from a fishing village to a futuristic world class city was on an unstoppable upward trajectory.

From Dubai, I had once-in-a-lifetime opportunities to visit Petra, Jordan's legendary Rose City, and three of Iran's most important cultural centres. There was food and drink on land and water to savour in Southern India, and an impromptu tasting session at a cookery school in Tbilisi, Georgia. I engineered a theatrical world premiere in the Middle East, witnessed superhuman performance art in Hobart, and marvelled at Kiev's fabulously eccentric toilet museum. Then there was that weird encounter on a Polish train and flying to New York to catch *Springsteen on Broadway*. My quirky collection of postcards includes these and many more – a veritable pick and mix of destinations, moods, favourite live performances, art, food, social comment, and the occasional bizarre experience. I hope you enjoy the ride.

Ruth Badley

1

From Yorkshire to Dubai?

If someone offered you the chance to move to another country for two or three years, how soon could you be ready to leave? What would you need to do before departure day? At the very least you might need to prepare family and friends for an emotional wrench. There is your current home to consider and the financial agreements you have in place with utilities, mortgage providers and insurance companies. Cars to sell, garden maintenance to arrange, the removal and storage of furniture to plan for. The older you are when the opportunity comes, the more there is to think about and for us that also extended to the two adult children we would be leaving behind.

'How would you feel if we moved to Dubai for a couple of years?' I threw the question into the air and held my breath. We'd arranged a family meeting at an East London pub to test the waters with our two sons. We were seeking their approval, I suppose. Were we being completely irresponsible? Would they be happy to see their parents relocate overseas, just like that?

'Fantastic, what an opportunity! Go for it!' The response, a wholehearted and unambiguous duet and for the rest of the evening we speculated on the amazing holidays they could have, as soon as we got settled.

We were not relocation novices at this point. In the early 1980s Tim worked in oil exploration and was offered a married posting to South Australia. No mobile phone communication. No email. No social media. Only thin, blue airmail letters and crackly landlines, but it was a lot easier to leave home in our twenties. Pack your bags and get on the plane. Three amazing years in Adelaide followed, with a couple of trips back home via Japan, Hong Kong, Thailand, Singapore and New Zealand.

Homesickness is a funny thing, and not just for your country of origin. I was homesick for Australia when we finally returned to the UK. The excitement of frequent overseas travel and discovery stopped for a while, but as soon as we could we were taking our two boys abroad for holidays.

We had been playing with the idea of having another adventure before retirement beckoned so when Dubai was suggested by Tim's employer, it was an easy decision. We were seasoned travellers. We knew how to do this. Pack our bags and get on the plane, right? Well not quite.

This time a houseful of possessions, amassed over twenty-six years of family life needed to be sorted through. We planned to rent out our Yorkshire home while we were away and an unfurnished let meant we needed to arrange storage for the things we were not taking with us.

As soon as we started on this task, I learned much more about the actual practicalities of relocating overseas, all the boring stuff that the expat forums don't tell you.

Having spent more than three decades building a home and a family in several places, the accumulation of stuff was staggering. Our friends marvelled at the amount of storage space we had in our house. The loft and the garage were standard issue but the additional cupboards, units and even complete rooms had been added over the years, largely out of the need to find a place to collect and keep more and more stuff.

One half of the partnership has trouble letting go of anything so the nostalgia value of much of the paraphernalia was immense, and consequently acted as something of a distraction during previous attempts to offload. Instead of getting rid it has been more a case of rearrange, but basically hang on to it all.

I should hold my hands up too. It was so much easier to consign a bunch of redundant possessions to a place where they were out of sight than spend precious time deciding what to do with every item. Little did I realise I was feeding a monster with an insatiable appetite.

So before our new life could get off the ground we had to get to grips with it. It was hard graft, both mentally and physically. The ultimate aim was house clearance. If we were not storing it or taking it with us, it needed to go – either to charity, another owner, or the bin. If you are looking to downsize or simply clear the clutter, what I learned could be helpful.

1. Break the task down into manageable and logical steps so you see progress.

2. Start with the smallest area and concentrate on the things you no longer want or use.

3. Make friends with the folk that manage the local tip, for guidance. Often there are charity collections on site, in addition to the standard recycling and disposal.

4. Do not do it alone. Enlist help with the children's rooms – from the children. Ours are adults but came back home to give invaluable assistance.

5. Accept that this task cannot be completed in a weekend and ensure all parties understand the magnitude of the undertaking. You need commitment to see it through.

6. Order a skip, but one size bigger than you think you'll need. Be prepared to order another. You *will* need it.

7. Ask relatives and friends, especially the hoarding kind to take some stuff off your hands. They will happily oblige. Partners tend to overlook the inconvenience because you are leaving the country and they want to be helpful.

8. If you have masses of unwanted books do not despair. Google the companies that take them for cash. They will often buy old CDs, DVDs and games too.

9. Get the hoarders to deal with selling items that have obvious value – they usually have the patience required to get results.

10. Enjoy the moment when you come across an object or document that is emotionally significant. It means you have

actually found something worth keeping in all the detritus. A
triumph!

2

Heavyweight Travellers

We finally whittled our possessions down to the items we wanted to keep, but did not need to set eyes on for two or three years. They filled six containers.

A storage facility in the depths of North Yorkshire added our consignment to their list. The contemporary artist, Michael Landy once famously turned all his possessions, and the deliberate disposal of same into an art work called *Break Down*. It seemed like madness at the time but I see what he was getting at now.

There is something altogether disturbing about packing your life away into so many boxes. Consumption takes on a new meaning when the volume is calculated, and every item in each box is wrapped, packed, sealed, and documented. Ownership becomes a responsibility and one that weighs heavy. So after weeks of preparation, when the van was packed and the load went on its way, it felt like we had finally tamed the beast and the path ahead was clear.

Actually, the path ahead was surprisingly clear. Clean, empty rooms. So much space and so easy to pack what we really needed to take with us. Do not get the idea we were travelling light, though. As if. Two enormous suitcases each, plus the biggest, niftiest hand luggage allowed.

We thought we were so clever just taking the essentials but the day before the big departure from Heathrow we had a pang. Maybe we ought to get the luggage weighed so we would be prepared for the cost, just in case we were a few kilos over the limit? Ouch.

I was ten kilos over, naturally, but hey, the casual packer in the partnership notched up a whopping fifteen kilos excess baggage. To add insult to injury, at check-in on different scales it turned out the original calculation was out by five kilos, so even more to pay on top. There were no bargains. The charges were eye-watering. If the relocation had been at our expense, trust me, we would have wept.

It was a sobering moment though, and one that signalled we would have to leave the Yorkshire thrift mentality behind. We were, after all, heading towards Dubai, the economic equivalent of cloud cuckoo land.

3

New Kids on the Dubai Block

It was only day two but the need to put down roots in our new location was overwhelming, so the search for an apartment began in earnest. The online guides to Dubai that formed part of my pre-travel research had not been particularly illuminating on the different residential areas. They all offered distinct pros and cons depending on your particular situation.

The Greens was an area that sounded promising but after an abortive visit, we learned that the kind of fully furnished accommodation that we had in mind was rarely on offer there.

On a recce trip three months back, we were immediately attracted to the area around Dubai Marina but the traffic congestion would likely make Tim's route to work a daily bind. A new tram service was exacerbating the problem, allowing vehicles to bank up while the tram proceeded across a main junction at about two miles an hour. Confident, savvy Dubai seemed to have installed a toy tram by mistake.

The Marina did have another important attraction for the new kids in town, though. It was there that we were first introduced to the redoubtable Julieta, the real estate agent, originally from Bulgaria, who would help, 'dear Ross and Tim' to find their ideal apartment.

Julieta was a remarkable multi-tasker. She drove, negotiated complex deals on the phone, and found addresses that were not yet on the map, whilst all the while relating tales of her experiences with awkward landlords to the two stunned Brits in the car that occasionally nodded in astonished agreement.

She used the word, "welcome" frequently. When she invited us to get in the lift or her car, we were always welcome, but god help the over–zealous security guard that stood in the way of a viewing, and her potential commission. Then it was, 'Don't be giving me this hassle,' delivered in an icy tone. Real estate agents in Dubai operate on a commission-only basis so they are like tigers circling their prey – and clients are lunch. Despite that, I liked Julieta. She spent a whole morning with us and thanks to her efficiency we viewed seven apartments. She left us at a café to mull over the two best options which were far from ideal. When the tiger leaves her prey unguarded, another will soon spot an opportunity.

The smart young man at the next table immediately noticed we were looking at accommodation details and offered to help us find a suitable property. What sort of thing were we looking for? Fully furnished in the Downtown area? Price range? No problem. He could show us one now, just over there. Arabian style. We might like it, he purred.

With our British sensibilities ruffled we stiffened. This had all the hallmarks of a scam. We should proceed with extreme caution. Under the table I quickly googled the company on the business card we demanded to see. Seemed to check out as legit. Actually, quite upmarket. He promised to return in half an hour with keys, and in the meantime Tim phoned a contact to double-check the company was to be trusted. Seemed it was reputable.

While we were waiting, the penny dropped. The apartment he had in mind was in Old Town, a unique low rise development, built to resemble an Arabian heritage village. It was surrounded by gleaming, shimmering, skyscraper tower blocks, only surpassed by the mighty Burj Khalifa landmark. All the apartments we had been shown up to this point were in the high rise glass towers, with views straight into other blocks or overlooking construction sites. We'd been told that furnished apartments in that more attractive heritage development we could see far below us were rarely available.

The young man, whose name was Farhad did return and delivered what others could not. A furnished apartment on the third floor of a small block in Old Town, with a Burj Khalifa view. It suited us perfectly. After picking over every tiny detail of the contract, (as we had been strongly advised to do, to avoid problems further down the line), the deal was completed.

So sorry, Julieta.

4

Footloose in the Mall

I was itching to move out of our tiny hotel room and into our apartment but we had to wait until Tim's residency visa and Emirates ID came through. In the meantime I decided to spend a day in Downtown to see what the Old Town development was like on an average day, and how I might fit in to the new surroundings. Was it even as attractive as I remembered?

Before I left the UK I'd started following interesting Dubai-based food businesses on Twitter so it was a bonus to find one of these located in the nearby souk. All the fresh salads, breads and cakes on display at *Baker & Spice* looked so inviting, plus they served great coffee. I really needed a friend to share it with though, and they didn't sell those there.

I would have plenty of opportunity to shop local, though. A farmer's market outlet, with lush green veg and tomatoes that looked as if they might have some flavour were on display in baskets outside the shop. An eager customer was inside filling her basket and so I met bubbly, friendly Monica from Sardinia. No, she didn't live on this development but close enough to shop for food most days. When in Dubai, shop for food like an Italian. Not a bad philosophy.

I had a wander round the residential area. Given that Dubai had been fashioned out of the desert, this area was surprisingly lush and green. It was quiet, and relaxing. An oasis in the heart of the city, but somehow shielded from the hubbub. I would have to take care not to spoil the peace by playing my favourite rock music.

Dubai Mall was within striking distance and the time had come to investigate this retail behemoth. I was on a mission to secure a reliable hairdresser and Monica had recommended one of the salons on my hit list. Opposite Waitrose, she advised.

Now there's Waitrose and then there is its much, showier cousin, Waitrose in Dubai. Pyramids of fruit perfection, polished and primped greet the casual passer-by through an open entrance, modelled on Harrods food hall. No tired, green plastic display areas here and because of religious sensitivities, the piggy products were housed in a secret pork shop at the back. I left without a purchase. No rush. l had two years to give them all the money I had for a pot of yoghurt.

Dubai certainly seemed a bonkers world as far as prices went. We joked before we arrived that Tim would spend two years saying, "Ow much?" in an incredulous Yorkshire accent, but even one given to regular extravagance (me) was taken aback by the cost of most things. I planned to conduct extensive research at the many shopping malls and souks, but on first impressions, and with some notable exceptions, such as petrol, most goods and services were about 1.5 times more expensive than in the UK.

Residential rents were stratospheric too and payable in advance for a whole year. To be able to negotiate at all, the full amount was required up front in a single payment. Instalments were possible but only in quarterly chunks and certainly not on a month in advance basis.

Taxis, we were told were still reasonable. Well, yes, cheaper than black cabs in London, but not so cheap that you didn't notice the cash disappearing if you relied on them to get you around, as we had during our first couple of weeks.

It was something of a surprise to find that licensed taxi drivers were not familiar with their patch. One refused to take us where we needed to go because he didn't know how to get there. Others might let hapless customers in the cab, clock up substantial amounts on the meter finding the way, or give up completely and dump passengers a long way from their desired destination. Nearness is a peculiar concept in Dubai. Saying something was near to, or even next to, could mean at least half a mile away. No fun for a pedestrian forced to walk in blistering heat along a non-existent pavement. We planned to lease a car as soon as possible. Petrol in Dubai was a giveaway, coming in at around thirty-three British pence per litre. Happy days.

The general rule of thumb on eating out was to expect it to be expensive for what you'd had and then a bit more on top. Salaries for professionals were high though, and with no deduction of income tax it was a fairly painless adjustment, once the first pay day came around. As a consequence, there was a ready market in the professional expat community who were generally willing and able to pay whatever it cost to eat, drink, and live in the style that their disposable income demanded.

Much of the leisure and social activity centred around the extravagantly appointed hotels across the city. Luxury became a meaningless description. Fantasy was more accurate. Arabian interior opulence reigned supreme, and even the names of the hotels were out of this world: *The One and Only Royal Mirage,*

The Address, Atlantis. The magnificent *Palace Hotel* just across the road from our apartment was already on my special occasion radar. It followed the winning Dubai formula. In brief, the more money and imagination you put into building a hotel, a shopping mall, or a landmark, the more people will want to be seen spending an excessive amount of money in it.

Which brings me back to the mall and the purchase of shoes. A girl in a new town always needs comfortable shoes but where to start? The sign in the mall pointed to The Shoe District. Christian Louboutin, Dolce & Gabbana, Chanel, Valentino, Gucci, Louis Vuitton. I could go on but you get the picture. There were American and European brands that were less familiar but equally top dollar. Beautiful designs but none that my feet would thank me for, never mind my wallet. I looked around much as I would an art gallery. It was interesting but I was yet to see a pair of shoes that real human beings could wear. A department store was surely the place.

I asked an assistant in Bloomingdales to tell me where I might find ordinary fashion shoes. I meant what we might think of as "high street," but feared that term could be confusing. Two big, beautiful brown eyes widened with incomprehension and just a trace of pity. She directed me to The Souk, an area of the mall where local traders sold ethnic Arabian clothing items, gold, jewellery and decorative slippers. Not really what I had in mind.

After what seemed like miles of traipsing round, I came upon a branded shoe shop I recognised. I nearly purchased, but held back because my feet were swollen from all the walking. Dubai Mall is equivalent in size to fifty soccer fields. Nothing for it, I would have to return. The search for shoes had only just begun.

5

A Taste for Local Knowledge

Holed up in a hotel for two weeks had brought some highs and lows on the eating front, particularly as we had been staying at one of Dubai's budget establishments on a bed, breakfast and dinner basis. We hadn't always taken dinner though. Two days in, we gave the dish of the day a whirl and what they did to a poor innocent piece of tuna scared us off. Overcooked, to the consistency of a rubber ball it was hard to believe it was once a fish. It was almost impossible to swallow which is quite a feat of achievement on the chef's part. Luckily, we could fill up on the salad buffet, which apart from an overcooked pasta creation, had been prepared with minimal interference from the kitchen.

On our second night we ventured out to an event run by a well-established worldwide organisation for expats. These evenings were an opportunity to meet people from all over the world and to put questions to more experienced residents. A German couple we met suggested we visit the Irish Village. They thought we would love it. Irish Village? Sounded like it could be a bit naff. On the map it looked like it was walking distance from our hotel, so we gave it a go.

Yes, it was an Irish-themed pub at heart but with a huge terrace area, live music and comfortingly familiar menu. It was relaxed, friendly and of course the warm evenings made it super popular with all nationalities and the occasional special guest. Bob Geldof played there on St Patrick's Day most years, we were told. That reminds me, hey Bob, when you're next in Dubai, I think this town could make serious steps towards making poverty history, don't you think?

For a traditional roast dinner, an Irish stew, or a pint of Guinness, this was definitely the place to come. We wolfed down the plate of roast lamb and all the trimmings with some pleasure. OK, the Yorkshire puddings were shop bought and the gravy was a little strange, but the sublime, creamy mash and perfectly cooked cauliflower and broccoli indicated that this chef was not only cooking with gas, he also knew when to turn it off. Always helpful.

The Irish Village was just one of a number of decent quality eating and drinking options we found on this site. The Italian and French restaurants we tried there on other nights were both good too. Just as well, as with Dubai's tennis arena also nearby, Andy Murray and the rest of the world's tennis darlings would be able to grab a quick bite during the Dubai Duty Free Tennis Championships they were advertising.

A foodie contact told me Dubai was curry heaven if you knew where to go. So true for Yorkshire too. Look for a good one in Harrogate and disappointment awaits. Local knowledge will always point you to curry perfection in nearby Leeds or Bradford. A work colleague of Tim's did us a massive favour by bringing us to *Ravi,* his favourite Dubai curry house, during our first fortnight.

The large frontage, set on a prominent corner indicated this was a well-loved business with a faithful clientele. Waiting staff carried laden trays from a tiny doorway at a constant pace. Locals were queuing for takeaways and the rough and ready tables, set up on the street outside were packed with diners of all nationalities. A little further along, through an open window we could see the fluffiest, freshest roti bread being shaped, rolled and cooked to order.

Maybe it was because I was exceptionally hungry, or perhaps it was the vibrant atmosphere but I would go as far as to say that this was one of the top curry experiences I have ever had. Mutton Handi, Chicken Ginger, Saag Aloo, Mutton Jalfrezi, a side dish of daal, and those sublime roti breads. Way too much food but all in the name of research. What impressed was the quality of the ingredients and the care in the preparation. Juicy, flavourful chicken and meltingly tender, properly trimmed lamb. Each dish had its own depth of flavour and the different spices, sauces and colours made every dip of the bread very moreish. At roughly £18 for three people, it was even cheaper than Leeds and Bradford. It didn't feel like Dubai at all!

6

Dubai's Desert Heart

Most questions about living in Dubai predictably concern the weather and how to cope with the extreme heat. They were the same ones I asked myself often enough before we arrived. We'd had a gentle start in February when daytime temperatures were agreeably warm, but there's more to Dubai than just unadulterated heat. There's wind and sandstorms too. Occasionally there's even rain which, much like snow in the UK, signals chaos on the roads because there is no drainage in the gutters, so the rain stays at surface level.

For the first three weeks of our arrival, Dubai put on its best welcome for two sun-starved Brits that blossomed in the warm glow of the UAE's winter temperatures. The need to even wonder about weather conditions seemed slightly ridiculous when every day brought uninterrupted sunshine and clear blue skies. We started to get confident. Big mistake.

Every so often Dubai stamps her foot to remind citizens that its futuristic cityscape and rampant consumerism are a veneer. Underneath the surface of glamour and glitz, Dubai has a restless, desert heart. Most of the time the fine, sandy dust in the air was kept in check by armies of workers that made sure the marbled mall floors and the streets in the swanky parts of town stayed in pristine condition. It was quite amazing how spotless and tidy it all was but every so often the forces of nature got the upper hand when the notorious desert winds blew in. Living in an apartment made me appreciate the amount of sweeping, polishing, and preening it took to keep signs of the desert at bay.

On one particularly stormy day, I wiped sandy dust from the glass-topped table on our balcony several times in an hour, finally giving up when a hazy fog reduced the city's skyline to a ghostly line-up.

The Burj Khalifa, usually such a strident presence was a shadow of its former self, its sold structure barely visible. Anyone with an expensive ticket to enjoy the panoramic view from the upper floors would have been cursing their bad luck.

On foot, we took a short cut below the mall, noting the layer of fine sand taking the shine off the Rolls Royces and Ferraris in the underground car park. Those still out on the street were scurrying along, holding scarves or masks over their faces. It felt like a deadly disease had just broken out. My skin felt gritty and I had a tickly sensation in my throat. Contact lens wearers and those with respiratory problems were compelled to take cover indoors until conditions improved.

Dubai offered its own solution of course, applicable in all weather conditions. If it's too hot, too windy or too dusty, don't worry. Go to the mall and shop.

7

Bling It On

Understated, subtle, restrained, and unadorned. Dubai does not understand these concepts, much less live by them. How very refreshing.

Perhaps it was something to do with the dazzling sunlight bouncing off the city's waterways and courtyard pools, or the way the glass and marble facades of the buildings appeared to glimmer in the heat of the day. Glitter and sparkle seemed almost natural elements and quite appealing to a Brit, recently arrived, with skin as pale as whitewash from too many Yorkshire winters.

Driving around after dark, the illuminations are spectacular. The Dubai Fountain alone uses more than six and a half thousand "superlights" and every building twinkles to attention after sundown. Even the palm trees put on their evening wear. It's attractive and exciting. It would be a tad ostentatious anywhere else, but somehow it all makes sense in Dubai.

It was about a month in when the ice-cold hands and feet the Yorkshire climate bestowed on me became a distant memory. I was reminded of this at night when I needed soap to remove the rings from my heat-swollen fingers. My feet were also complaining about being squeezed into summer sandals that all of a sudden seemed a size too small, and rather dull. I had acquired the attention span of a magpie. Shiny, sparkly embellished footwear was everywhere and my feet felt like frumps.

My first foray into Dubai Mall was definitely over-ambitious. The big mistake was trying to cover too much ground in an afternoon and without a map. Even *with* a map, my sense of direction, or lack of it, took me down some blind alleys. Mission bling was never going to be easy with my feet.

Eventually, and somewhat breathless I reached the target outlet and located objects of desire that would please my hard done by hoofs.

The service was immaculate. I got the full Cinderella treatment, meaning the assistant was more than willing to stretch the chosen pairs, so I could leave the shop feeling like they were made for my not so dainty plates. Yes, two pairs. A girl's gotta have plenty of bling to feel at home in Dubai.

8

Let's Do Brunch!

The concept of Friday brunch is part of the Dubai lifestyle. It's a leisure activity, a cultural event, and the mainstay of the hospitality industry. It's also a very enjoyable way to share food with friends. Pretty much every restaurant, hotel and bar embraces the concept, putting their own spin on what is generally an eat and drink package, designed to satisfy the largest of appetites.

The working week in the United Arab Emirates is Sunday to Thursday. I thought it would take me ages to get used to thinking of Sunday as a working day. Not a problem. I found you can take pretty much anything in your stride when the sun is shining. If anything, the weekends seemed to come round a bit faster, and the Thursday night traffic suggested that employees would like to get their weekend underway even sooner, if only they could get to their destination in time for the party.

Friday is the Islamic day of prayer in the same way that Sunday is a religious day in the UK. For the majority of expats in Dubai, Fridays are devoted to enjoying a long, lazy brunch in the sumptuous surroundings of one of the many upmarket hotels. Extravagant, excessive, and a culinary experience I couldn't wait to try. If Friday was going to be the new Sunday, then I was all for brunch as the new lunch.

As luck would have it, we lived opposite the *Palace Hotel* which reputedly offered one of the best Friday brunches to be had in Dubai. It had to be sampled. Introduce, the all-you-can-eat-and-drink scenario, and with the best will in the world you will attract a variety of human life. It was a fascinating afternoon. We watched the behaviour of a table of French expats slowly deteriorate as the alcohol package they'd chosen started to take effect. More and more food piled up uneaten, while the liquid supplies were replenished with alarming speed and the volume of their banter increased. They were hard to ignore but were nevertheless a welcome distraction from the Emirati family that arrived soon after us. A mum, dad and two young children, out for a fancy brunch with a nanny in tow, at first sight appeared innocuous enough, until they sat down. Then it became uncomfortably clear that the Filipina nanny was not invited along to share the meal but only to supervise the children. There was no place setting or chair for the poor girl who had to stand watching until the rest of the family had eaten the equivalent of their own body weight.

The catering team at the hotel must have been expecting the population of a small country to turn up. There were dishes representing most of the world's major cuisines; fresh seafood, including an oyster bar; roasted and braised meats, with all the classic sauces and sides; every possible version of salad, and an outdoor grill and barbecue station where a brigade of chefs prepared mountains of scallops, lobster and the finest cuts of steak to order.

There were baskets of different breads, row after row of handmade desserts and patisserie and a selection of cheeses I didn't have room to even consider. I don't think I actually saw everything available and if I had tried to do so, there would have been no time to eat. In short, there was so much to tempt and satisfy that further exploration was hardly necessary. All the dishes were constantly replenished so there were no sad and sorry last knockings on show if diners turned up mid-afternoon. It was awesome and I don't use that word very often. A battalion of smiling waiters and chefs were on hand to minister to your every whim. Heck, if you fancied candy floss on a stick, you could have it. There was a chef, spinning the stuff. I kid you not.

9

Stressful Route to Relaxation

I made a promise to myself at the start of this journey, that I would explore the opportunities Dubai offered for self-improvement.

I have never been a great one for taking exercise. I don't remember the last time I broke into a run – probably around 1978 if I'm honest, when I was a teacher. Letting three dozen teenage boys arrive at the school hall ahead of time for their weekly drama lesson would have spelt disaster so I must have had the ability to put on a sprint at some point.

I'm told my walking speed is painfully slow, though I can pick up the pace considerably with only fifteen minutes left before Happy Hour is over.

Running, jogging, the gym and all the other stuff that either makes you wet, sweat or shed tears is not my idea of fun. Some twinges in the back, probably caused by too many hours hunched over a computer suggested that maybe it was time to consider some gentle stretching and strengthening routines. Pilates had been mooted. Yes, I thought. That's what I will explore in Dubai as part of my manifesto for a new and better me.

I already had an image in my mind of the imaginary Pilates class I was going to join. A large airy studio with scented candles strategically placed along the floor. The low tone of a relaxation soundtrack on a permanent loop, and a dozen devotees stretched out on floor mats, diligently concentrating on their breathing. My sort of exercise.

I did my research. The Mantra Fitness Club had me with the name and it was a short taxi ride away. It seemed altogether more appealing than the huge Fitness First right on our doorstep. At dusk, from our balcony we could hear one of the Australian trainers barking out commands and aggressive encouragement. It all sounded a bit too earnest for my liking, and signing up for a class right next door to our apartment seemed a cop out. No, it had to be the Mantra Fitness Club. Not Pilates but Yogalates was the offer. Sounded pretty. I'll give it a go.

There was a taxi rank just steps away, so with ample time allowed for travel, I told the driver where I needed to go and prepared to hop in. Not so fast. Puzzled looks. Shaking of head. Doesn't know the location. OK, had this before. Dubai is such a fast growing city that new roads, tower blocks and business locations often leave the taxi drivers behind. When the same scene played out another three times, I sensed something weird was going on. The taxi rank was outside a smart hotel so I asked one of the doormen if he could assist. He knew exactly where I needed to go and he also knew why I was having a problem.

The journey would only clock up a paltry fifteen dirhams (less than £3) on the meter. The drivers, he told me are *pretending* they don't know where you want to go because they want to bag a more lucrative fare. He had a cunning plan, though. He asked a colleague in the hotel to google the location and print out a map. Give the taxi driver a picture of the route and he will have no option but to take you there, said my oh-so-confident ally.

Armed with the map and with Mr Confident in tow we hailed the next cab. I said where I wanted to go, smugly produced my map as the protests of ignorance began, and hopped in the back. An argument then ensued between the taxi driver and Mr Confident. I could still hear them as I put the map in my bag and slipped out of the taxi to try my luck with the next one in the queue. Time was ticking by. My class started in twenty minutes.

This time I tried a different tack. I explained that half a dozen taxi drivers had already refused to take me where I needed to go, so what was I supposed to do? I struck lucky because this one spoke excellent English. He genuinely didn't know the location but was happy to use my map to get me there. We chatted about London cab drivers and The Knowledge. He agreed that it was all a bit of a shambles in Dubai because there was so much pressure on the drivers to exceed a daily business target. He wished he could be a taxi driver in London because he thought the priorities in Dubai were all wrong. The managers were only concerned about making money. The drivers knew they wouldn't hit their targets if they picked up too many fifteen dirham fares in a day, so they went through this elaborate pantomime to avoid them. He was a lovely guy and I gave him a decent tip for filling me in on the realities, and getting me to the Ontario Tower with five minutes to spare.

The reception area was manned by the usual security bod who mumbled directions whilst pointing at the lift. I thought I heard him say something about a car park but dismissed this as irrelevant information. No, he did actually mean IN the car park. There was no signage at all. I asked someone else, a little more urgently and she pointed a finger round a hidden corner.

Ironically, I broke into a run. The Mantra Fitness Club was basically a couple of rooms inside a multi-storey car park.

I was out of breath and panicky because I was late, and not used to running. I could hear a chanting soundtrack and beyond the reception area glimpsed a studio and candles! There didn't seem to be any students, though. A tiny Indian woman with thick glasses was manning the reception desk.

'Do you get many coming here for classes?' I ventured.

'Not really.' I started giving her my thoughts on why that might be and how stressful it had been to find the place, what with the taxis and then no directions to guide the visitor, but stopped mid-sentence because I sounded, well, a bit British. She nodded in sympathy and smiled knowingly.

With my small reserves of stamina now depleted I gave the class my best shot. I couldn't complain. I was the only student so I had one-to-one coaching in the moves and excellent advice from a patient instructor.

'You need a beginner's class and a lot of individual supervision,' he said. 'Actually I know a really good Pilates class for you and it is right where you live, so very convenient. Fitness First. Say I sent you.'

10

Bob G and Jack D in Dubai

Back in the UK, I had no idea how many acts put Dubai on their tour schedule. Living in Dubai, I wished more did. My favourite live performer being a case in point.

All the time I was in Dubai I kept a careful ear to the ground for any news of a Bruce Springsteen tour to Europe. My dreams would eventually come to fruition, but word had already gone round that it would be at least another year before Bruce would be on the road. So I had a huge gap in my live music addiction to fill. Tim's guitars were yet to arrive from the UK, and until they did, he'd find it tricky to join a band. Air guitar could only get you so far.

Soon after we arrived we heard that Bob Geldof would be making his annual St Patrick's Day pilgrimage to Dubai to perform at the Irish Village, a haven for expats dreaming of drinking a pint of Guinness in their summer clothes. So we'd booked tickets and were standing in reverence, awaiting the headline act, not quite at the front of the stage as I try to be for Bruce, but near enough to feel involved and quite excited.

I was never a huge fan of the Boomtown Rats, though the obvious charisma of the lead singer and his most famous composition, inspired by a schoolgirl's shooting rampage, gave them massive cred. All Bob Geldof's subsequent achievements and personal losses hijacked his original career as a singer/songwriter, so this gig was a bit of an eye-opener as to what might have been.

The monumental family tragedies, all painfully played out in the public arena required him to be a very present father to several daughters, and no doubt had an impact on his musical activity. No wonder then, that with unkempt hair a whiter shade of pale, and a sharp business suit instead of unwashed jeans, the elder statesman of punk admitted that these days THAT song is the only reason he still gets any f****ing gigs at all.

As far as celebrity campaigners go, Geldof is an icon. Band Aid, Live Aid and his eloquent and vociferous efforts to engage decision makers on the issues of poverty, famine relief and Ebola, have kept him in the public eye. During his Dubai concert, he veered effortlessly from rock to reggae to an Irish knees-up. One song, written when he returned to Ethiopia some years after the famine, and when he was going through a bad phase in his own life, was particularly poignant. The backstory to it centred on those he met, the simple food they shared, and the success of a project funded by Live Aid, giving the villagers the means to grow different crops. The experience, he said, was transformative.

The voice, eerily like Dylan on some songs, notably the touching *Dazzled by You,* could also still rock it for *Mary of the Fourth Form* and deliver the attitude required for *Rat Trap.* Minutes later he was orchestrating the audience in a hi-diddly-di-singalong in honour of St Patrick. I never knew Bob Geldof was so versatile. The stage presence was never in doubt and was still there in bucketloads.

He had the good sense to surround himself with a band of outstanding musicians, including the lead guitarist, who performed some blistering solos in comparison to Bob's pedestrian strumming. It was Tim who spotted that Bob played his guitar upside down, an acknowledged fact amongst guitar aficionados. The violin and mandolin player cut a workmanlike dash, when he stripped down to his vest, but boy could the man *play*.

We were all waiting for THAT song and wisely it came mid-set, just when we least expected it. A song, written in 1979 about the banality that fuelled a US school shooting is as relevant today as it ever was. Singing back the words to *I Don't Like Mondays* to Bob Geldof was pretty special. That'll do till Bruce calls.

I wondered how long into the gig it would be before either Josh Widdicombe or Jack Dee mentioned tax-free earnings to the sell-out crowd at Dubai's World Trade Centre. It was rather further in to Jack Dee's peerless set than expected but it was a relief when it came all the same. You can't call yourself a comedian, come to Dubai and fail to heckle the mostly British audience on that point. If you happened to have Jack Dee's talent for turning grouchiness into an art form then so much the better.

By its nature, stand-up comedy doesn't easily stretch to a whole evening format. It seemed an age before the young pretender, Josh Widdicombe bounded on for half an hour of his well-worn material on Devon, his mum's protective attitude to wheelie bins, Coco Pops, homemade jam, and the lamentable performance of the battery in his mobile phone.

The trademark, high-pitched payoff lines worked their magic well enough but somehow it all seemed a bit too predictable. I would have been more impressed if he had sought to challenge himself with new and specific observations, geared to the Dubai crowd. For a funny guy that specialises in being constantly incredulous he couldn't have landed in a better place. Shame he didn't mine it for all it was worth to give us a couple of new thoughts during his thirty minutes on stage. Given the comfort level of the seats at this venue, it was fortunate that an extended interval preceded the headline act. I suspect this tactic was designed to fool us into thinking we were getting a full evening's entertainment.

The first unscripted observation from Jack Dee was spot on. The venue *did* resemble the interior of a warehouse and was just as welcoming! The scripted material, delivered from the picture-of-misery face that is Dee's calling card was a series of extended and often rambling tales of woe, peppered with some dry and witty observations on the Dubai Mall and the misuse of the term "expat," when "immigrant" was surely more appropriate.

The characteristic bad week he was having was the hook to hang extended riffs on the electricity supply, adolescence, giving directions to strangers, taxi drivers, and set pieces on family life that anyone familiar with his Lead Balloon series would recognise.

A consummate professional at the top of his game, Dee had mastered the performer's art of deception. With all the backtracking and going off at tangents it appeared as if these thoughts were occurring to him for the first time. I was ready to believe that if I caught him on another night his stories would be different.

No one could accuse Jack Dee of rushing on and off. A full hour and half on stage, and possibly a minute or two more than he planned, thanks to the pesky fly that got in on the act, mid-tale. If the seats had been more comfortable I would definitely have been shouting for more.

11

Brunch at the Billion Pound Hotel

Before we made the decision to move to Dubai we came over for a week, for the purpose of checking the place out. It was during that first trip that the symbol of the city, the stunning Burj Al Arab hotel, cast a spell. Its photogenic ship's sail exterior was all over the pages of the flight magazines and it kept bobbing into view on the skyline during that first visit. When we checked into our somewhat less exclusive hotel we discovered that the rooftop bar afforded a tantalising view of this iconic structure.

In our extreme ignorance and naivety we thought a drink at this landmark ought to be on the list of experiences that first week, and would be the perfect location to give the whole relocation idea some serious thought. So we put on some smartish gear, got our hotel to arrange a taxi and off we went. Half an hour later we were back in the lobby of our hotel, thirst unquenched, but armed with some useful information about how getting in to this hotel actually works.

You can't just rock up for a drink, or anything else for that matter. This is the mothership of exclusivity. Of course, the British know all about keeping the riff-raff out. Our infamous class system bestows all sorts of life's advantages on the upper echelons in our society, while keeping the less privileged firmly in their place. If you think it was snobbery that prevented us from getting a drink there that night you would be wrong. True, we were a bit miffed at the time but since moving here, I know what was going on.

What seemed to be everything to do with high class gatekeeping was actually more about providing top class service. They need to know you are expected, so they can roll out the red carpet. Reservations have to be made – even for a drink – so your name is on the guest list. The Burj Al Arab, a bit like my deceased grandma, demanded to have advanced notice of your arrival, to make sure the fridge was full and the best tea set was on the table.

There was no hint of condescension or snootiness when we turned up without an invite, as there might be in the UK. A revealing television documentary showed that the staff may be used to revamping the gold leaf chair legs for big spenders and royalty, but apply exactly the same standards if Mr and Mrs Ordinary arrive for their Special Treat.

Having been denied access the first time, naturally made the whole experience ten times more desirable. Tim's birthday offered the perfect reason to go for it. Friday brunch was just about affordable coming in at just shy of £150 each.

No hitches as we were waved through security and across the bridge to the small private island and valet parking, signalling that this time, our names were on the magic list. The lobby was designed to deliver the wow factor and the water features, sculptured ceilings, and the towering golden opulence of the interior structure kept us gawping as the escalator propelled us ever upwards.

Unfortunately, there was no opportunity to wander off the beaten track, to glimpse an open door or look round a suite. There are no mere rooms – only suites. I asked if we could have a look at one. Responding with extreme politeness, the answer was no because nothing must disturb the privacy of the hotel's guests. Finding two nosey Brits having a butchers at the end of your corridor was simply not the Burj Al Arab way.

The escalator revealed another glittering lobby, where a waiting elevator silently beamed us up to the welcoming committee at the *Al Muntaha* restaurant on the 27th floor.

The interior design, with its show-off peacock tail blues and greens was in perfect harmony with the sea and skyscape panorama. The view from the ocean shore through to the science fiction outline of Downtown is immense, so no surprise that window seats in the restaurant were in high demand. We hadn't booked one, but one was found nevertheless.

It was unexpected, but a welcome touch to be offered a complementary glass of prosecco with brunch. Not just an ordinary glass of prosecco, either. A Bellini. They know how to please at this joint.

Brunch had the fine dining refinement I'd anticipated, with several extra bells and whistles. On one side of the room, dish after dish of elegantly presented European and Middle Eastern starters and salads cried out for attention. I made an immediate connection with the shot glasses of avocado and green apple soup, garnished with a juicy cube of marinated salmon and caviar cream. Superb.

Other highlights included the risotto station where chef was creating individual portions to order; an enticing selection of fish and vegetables in tempura batter; a display of half a dozen kinds of caviar; a seafood and sushi bar; Indian and Arabian meat and fish dishes, and European-style slow cooked duck and lamb. Ample choice, and whist the tempura could have been a little crispier everything else we tried was tip top. Just when we thought a pause before dessert would be in order, the doors to the kitchen parted with a theatrical flourish and a waiter appeared wheeling a silver trolley of roast sirloin of beef. It arrived at our table, ready to be carved to order, so it would have been rude to turn it down, right? The curiously shaped Yorkshire puddings that accompanied the meat were a talking point and chef was certainly surprised to learn Yorkshire was a place. Was it a city? Well no, more a region. Is it in Europe? Looks like Yorkshire still has some work to do on the global marketing front.

A good quarter of the room was allocated to desserts and patisserie and even if we hadn't kept a tiny space in reserve, resistance was useless. Everything appeared cunningly dainty in size, a good encouragement to keep on sampling. From the pretty as a picture macarons to mini cheesecakes, cups of tiramisu to tiny vanilla slices, it was faultless. My favourite was the yuzu layer cake, the citrus-like topping cutting through the richness. Lifting the lid on a gleaming tureen I marvelled at the undisturbed contents. A bread and butter pudding, clearly there to ease the hunger pangs that might set in before the coffee arrived.

Service, it goes without saying, was exemplary. It would have been a wonderful experience even without the white box given to the birthday boy to take home, but what a charming touch. A branded chocolate birthday cake. Layers of the lightest sponge and chocolate mousse, presented as a gift ensured this brunch exceeded all expectation.

12

Chickens, Hens, Eggs and Chocolate

My title might suggest an Easter theme but I am not about to riff on new beginnings, rebirth, fluffy animals or indeed, chocolate.

The best food in Dubai is not always to be found in the swanky places with pretentious descriptions of basic dishes. Too often it turns out to be a case of style over substance. A straightforward form of words can also disappoint as these can lull you into thinking you will get exactly what you ordered. Too late you realise that chef, in a burst of madcap inspiration, culinary genius that he is, has deconstructed your favourite dessert. The clues were there after all. I might have guessed that passion fruit and yuzu cheesecake sounded too good to be true.

When the waiter leaned in, eyes reverently lifted skywards, whispering that chef's signature dish was not a traditional interpretation, my internal dessert alarm went to red alert.

It arrived. A creamy white chocolate sphere, placed over a ubiquitous smear of what I assume correctly is passion fruit puree. Smears are a particularly unpleasant trend and one that has been with us for far too long. They are so ungenerous for a start. Give me a proper taste of what it is, or don't bother. Just wiping a knife across a plate cannot be regarded as a legitimate addition to any dish.

Back to this peculiar looking sphere. Was this the cheesecake bit? Not from an initial prod of the fork as it seemed strangely unyielding. I looked round the dining room, wondering how I was going to eat this dessert without it bouncing off my plate and into someone else's lap. All the cheesecake loveliness must be inside, so I really needed to crack this, literally. No one in the kitchen had thought of the customer experience so there was only one option. I held my breath, hoped for the best and bashed my dessert with a spoon.

The cleverness was revealed in the passion fruit and yuzu sorbets mimicking the yolk and white of an egg. A refreshing and fragrant foil to the white chocolate sweetness. It was pleasant enough but a pointless pretender to the cheesecake crown. Those who love cheesecake would surely be deeply disappointed by this, and cheesecake haters would not have ordered it. Lose, lose.

I was developing an interesting, we-welcome-your-feedback kind of relationship with this particular venue so it would be unfair to name names, but some of their menu descriptions were odd to say the least. Witness the Dish of the Day. To mere mortals it was a chicken breast, probably nestling on a bed of whatever. I didn't get to hear the rest because I was too busy asking the waiter to repeat what sounded like stand-up comedy material. The dish of the day is a hen's breast? Is he having a laugh? No, this nonsense was alive and clucking in a Dubai kitchen, where stating the gender of the chicken was deemed critical to your eating experience.

I asked Twitter whether such information was justified on any level. Suppose I set my heart on rooster breast? What then? The chef, writer and broadcaster Rachel Khoo helpfully pointed out that roosters are slaughtered when older and are therefore tougher. So does stating the gender of the bird make the dish sound more appealing? More interesting? Or simply weird?

It turns out New York Times food blogger, Frank Bruni also thinks such verbose language is a touch precious and wrestled with this issue some time ago in relation to the hen's egg.

Male or female, the chicken I want to buy, cook and eat is the one reared with care and compassion and preferably in the locality. Tricky business in Dubai where everything is flown in, and locally grown and reared produce is harder to come by. I had been investigating my options on chickens and eggs as it is often hard to know exactly what you are buying in Dubai. Free range, organic chickens are available in selected supermarkets. They taste great but they come all the way from France. Tiny, locally reared organic chickens were sometimes available at our local farmer's market shop.

I was also alerted to *Greenheart*, an inspirational organic farm and shop selling their own fruit, vegetables, herbs, honey, cheese, and exceptionally tasty free range eggs.

The farm's website said that their chickens, hatched at the farm through several generations, live in large open-air enclosures shaded by trees, with space for the birds to run around. At night they slept in fanned and comfortable barasti huts made of natural materials and dined on a natural diet of grass and vegetables. Contented with these arrangements, the hens (obviously) produced small, white-shelled eggs with a delicious, rich orange yolk. So good when lightly poached and served on a slice of decent bread!

From a ridiculous menu to a sublime eating experience. It had been an eventful week.

13

Slow Boat to Dubai

Nearly three months had passed since a section of our front room back in Harrogate resembled a dumping ground. A collection of random household objects had been piled up in preparation for a journey into the unknown. The removal firm told us that shipping would take five weeks max, so we should provide a delivery address soon after our arrival.

As we had left home with no fixed abode in Dubai, we had visions of the whole lot arriving whilst we were still residing in a small hotel room. With that thought in mind there was no time to waste before getting ourselves settled into a suitable apartment. We needn't have worried.

Five weeks came and went and another five went by before we found out that our shipment was taking a different route and was going to Sohar, in Oman. Over the phone and true to form, the head of the removal firm in Yorkshire groaned at the apparent stupidity of our questions. Didn't we know that docking in a port, two hours away from Dubai was saving time on delivery? Hang on, saving time?

In the end, even the local agent's estimation went out of the window and all of a sudden we had a call to say our shipment would be delivered by one person, in the next hour. On the dot the doorbell rang and in he came, wheeling our boxes, followed by one, two, three, four – no less than eight guys – to assist with unpacking. With so many hands it was all done in a trice and we were left staring in wonder at the good and bad decisions we had made in January when we didn't have much of a clue about what we needed to bring and what we REALLY needed to bring.

We knew we wanted to rent a furnished apartment in Dubai and the fact that the basics were in place from the start was a huge help. We listened in alarm as others told us how they spent weeks on the floor of an empty flat as they worked their way through a long shopping list to ensure they could sleep, eat and shower in comfort. No thanks. Luckily, we had the foresight to anticipate what an unfurnished apartment might mean in reality.

What we should have realised is that furnished in name can also prove to be unfit for purpose and in hideous taste. The dining room table and chairs we found waiting for us was one such example. A circular table in a rectangular space, and made of such dark wood we needed the light on in the day just to see what we were eating. It was miserable to look at and the chairs were guaranteed to cause acute back problems. They had to go. On the upside, the bed in the main bedroom was vast and beautifully comfortable. I could forgive a lot of things, after a good night's sleep.

The kitchen was well designed with lots of storage. Someone in the recent past had nipped to IKEA and filled their trolley with the kind of stuff students in their first year at university might find helpful. Cheap and cheerful pots and pans, not designed for a lifetime's service, plus a selection of implements that seemed to suggest rudimentary cooking might be possible. A knife block contained four knives of varying sizes but all failed to cut through anything tougher than butter. With one all-purpose cooking tray and no oven-to-tableware, serving a meal with any sort of grace was a challenge at first. No longer. We were back to full service when the decent knives, sturdy saucepans, the pressure cooker, roasting tins, and several oven-proof dishes arrived.

We had been a bit fanciful with some of the items we thought we would need and others were simply comfort blankets. Why else would I believe Delia's Smith's cookery books would be so essential to a new life in Dubai?

Lamps are always useful to add mood and contrast to a living space and I'd been mentally placing several in focal points in the apartment for weeks. Packing seven was perhaps a bit over the top, particularly as bedside lamps were provided, but who knew?

Here's a selection of our good, and not so good packing decisions.

Good decisions

Not dragging bedding from home over here – ours would not have been anywhere near the right size for this gigantic bed.

Including teapots of assorted sizes, favourite mugs and a supply of teas.

Packing Sellotape, screwdriver, torches and extension leads, unglamorous but useful items that help to solve niggling domestic issues quickly.

A couple of framed pictures to instantly transform a rented apartment into our own space.

Not so good decisions

Shipping vast quantities of toiletries as most brands are available.

Including Tim's heavy towelling dressing gown and two of my thickest cardigans. Back in Yorkshire we obviously couldn't conceive of living in a place where every day was a hot one.

Not bringing the small wooden stepladder that would have helped me reach the top cupboards in the kitchen and bedroom.

Failing to include a single cake tin. Baking in air-conditioned comfort is the thing to do when it's too hot to go out!

14

The Three-Month Review

Three months in Dubai felt about the right amount of time to take stock of where we were with the settling in process. How do you know when a place feels like home and what are the significant factors that help new arrivals feel at one with a different culture?

By its nature, Dubai is a place that attracts expats from all over the world. A melting pot is a clichéd and somewhat inaccurate description of multicultural societies generally but in Dubai, particularly so. I loved living in a place that welcomed so many different nationalities but when you are new it is only natural to gravitate towards those that share your background. It was sobering to find that most Brits we met were a good deal younger than us, and for that reason we didn't always share the same cultural references.

The cleaner was from the Philippines, my hairdresser Lebanese and the maintenance guys for our apartment were Indian. In the previous month I'd lunched with a Korean, read books and plays with women from Tunisia, Australia, Wales, the USA, Northern and Southern Ireland, and met visual artists from France, Russia, Germany, and the UAE.

I did not have any sense that Emiratis complained about immigration to their country as certain groups in the UK do. Cultural richness, diversity, not to mention useful skills and cheap labour were welcome as long as local laws, religious observances and customs were respected. As a guest in Dubai, this was not hard to do.

Drinking alcohol in public is not allowed, but that doesn't mean you can't drink alcohol. Drunken behaviour on the street is not tolerated, though I can't help feeling that it would be a good thing if the UK was a tad less accepting of this kind of thing too. Freedom to witness fellow citizens collapsing on the pavement, vomiting into the gutter in a state of undress is not a freedom I cherish.

As a woman I felt completely safe walking around on my own after dark in Dubai. True, I lived in a very central and brightly lit area but nevertheless the statistics showed that the UAE has the world's lowest violent crime rate. Whilst Westerners may think otherwise, women are highly respected in this society. I had no concerns for my safety or security, and as a new arrival that was comforting.

For the first couple of months, life in Dubai was much less about feelings though and much more about processes. Some rather dull and lengthy ones actually. First, to obtain a residency visa and then the Emirates ID – the key to the magic kingdom. No one really exists until these documents have been issued, received, and can be produced on demand. One of the many stages on the road to recognition required a photo and fingerprints. When Tim showed up at the relevant office to do this he had to negotiate a disorganised queuing system, along with hundreds of other men, whilst I was ushered through to a separate area where just two or three women waited in a haven of calm and serenity. In situations like this, respect for women is tangible.

The other essential was a local mobile phone. Every transaction, from booking a restaurant to withdrawing money from a bank account was confirmed and recorded by a text message, in a way that would feel oppressive in the UK, but was actually quite useful. Invariably, a cash purchase in a shop prompted the sales staff to ask for your mobile number so they could bombard you with marketing guff. Data protection was not a readily understood and accepted concept. Opening a bank account though, was a whole other story. As a freelance worker I had no salary certificate issued by an employer, so my husband was required to vouch for me. Ouch!

Surprisingly, in 2015 many Dubai businesses lacked a credible website presence. Information was often out of date and the general user-experience was clunky and unreliable, leaving the customer frustrated and ill-informed. We quickly learned to always ring to make restaurant bookings as it was often the case that new internal processes were established that bypassed the website altogether.

I knew where to go to find most things I needed, apart from the post office which continued to elude me. I never thought I would miss the British postal delivery system and all its associated services but I did, greatly.

When we had a night out in another part of the city, returning to Downtown felt like going home but ultimately it was friendships that helped me make that leap.

On the street near our apartment I spotted someone I knew from the book group I'd joined. Actually, she recognised me first and waved. We stopped and chatted for a bit about work, books, and the next meeting and then we went about the rest of our day. Suddenly, I felt less of a stranger in town. Small steps.

15

Where's My Tribe?

There are obvious exceptions to this way of thinking, but being voluntarily plucked from everything and everyone you know and dropped in a new location, at least once in your life is no bad thing. The disruption really makes you think about who you are and what makes you tick. Exchanging predictable outcomes for a life lived in the moment is challenging but like most things worth doing, the more you put in, the greater the gain.

Despite the high numbers of expats all wanting to meet others in the same situation, making friends in Dubai was not that easy. As a freelancer working from home I didn't have co-workers to get to know. If you had small children or walked a dog, making contact with other parents and pet owners was in theory, more straightforward. I could see from my own neighbourhood that childminding and dog walking duties were often farmed out to others and in those cases it was the nannies and carers that tended to form friendships.

We lived in a residential complex with hundreds of apartments, yet it was months before we exchanged pleasantries with our Australian neighbour. Employees work long hours and play hard so were not necessarily at home at predictable times. On our floor there were many different nationalities but it's not appropriate in every culture to knock on the door and introduce yourself.

I concluded the only way to meet like-minded people was to plunge right in and get involved in activities I enjoyed doing. As soon as I did I found that those I wanted to connect with were right on my doorstep. I hadn't had to go out of my way to make new friends for a long time so it was a little daunting to suddenly think about thrusting myself into an established social scene in a different country.

Expat society in Dubai is transitory which could explain why folk generally seemed less committed to maintaining friendships in the way they might in their home country. Expats like ourselves were in Dubai for a defined amount of time. Obtaining residency, when we were there, was conditional on employment, unless you had sponsorship from a working spouse. Even those who came for a limited time and decided to stay had to leave before retirement. That explained why there were no elderly expats.

Inevitably, there were cliques in certain parts of town where ostentatious spending and endless pampering passed the time, but this was never going to be a sustainable way to make meaningful and lasting friendships.

As an avid reader, with more time to contribute to a book group, I thought this might be a good place to start. The online Meetup concept is great for this and the site indicated there was a book group right in my part of town, plus I was familiar with the book they planned to discuss at their next meeting.

I looked at the members' photos, picked two that looked friendly and decided to email them ahead of the meeting and introduce myself.

Emails swiftly translated to coffees, lunches, evenings out and invites to homes. By an amazing stroke of luck one of my new friends was a qualified Pilates instructor. She decided to take me on in her spare time and we found a suitable outdoor area for our weekly sessions. I began to enjoy early morning Pilates in the park, and my encouraging teacher told me I was making progress.

Another new friend told me she was a chef, so lots in common there, with Dubai's vibrant dining out culture to discover, and a mutual interest in cooking and eating great food. What else was I passionate about that required participation? Theatre.

I'd discovered the Dubai International Writers Centre, a newer addition to the local arts scene, located in an interesting heritage area of town. Volunteer actors were being sought to take part in script-in-hand readings of plays, written by the students of a playwriting course. I could do that. I would LOVE to do that. I emailed the organiser and received a positive response within the hour. Rehearsals on a Saturday afternoon and a performance the same evening.

Would I still be able to channel my inner drama queen? What if I made a complete fool of myself? I didn't have time to ponder on these issues or I might have pulled out. I'm so glad I didn't.

The plays covered fertile dramatic ground, from family secrets, mental health issues, to abusive relationships and magical realism. In an atmospheric courtyard setting, a scratch company, comprising teachers, a financial journalist, students of all ages, as well as writing and acting professionals put on a show for an invited audience. The idea was to give the playwrights a sense of how their work would translate to the stage.

I was fortunate to be cast in the only comedy, an amusing story charting the employees of a newly established international school, located in the aptly named Empty Quarter. This is an area where new arrivals usually go to experience the desert and much of what the trusty camel has to offer.

Four years' training at the Central School of Speech and Drama were poured into bringing a jobsworth school secretary off the page. A more subtle challenge, thrown down by the youngest playwright, aged twelve, was the role of a rabbit that relied on the powers of a golden acorn to maintain her intelligence.

If someone had told me that Dubai offered this kind of opportunity I would never have believed it. Wasn't it all about business and shopping? Dubai's exciting artistic and cultural scene gave the Emirate plenty more to shout about.

16

Theatre in a Nutshell

If ever there was a case of less is more, then the concept of the ten-minute play must be a worthy contender. I say this as one who has sat without complaint through her fair share of three-act dramas, whilst those around me grew ever more restless in their seats, hoping in vain for an early release back into the free world.

Dubai's annual Short+Sweet Festival of Theatre is the antidote to all that. A menu of varied theatrical nuggets, freshly crafted and energetically presented is a winning way to keep an audience involved and alert. If you don't like the play, chill out, there'll be another one along in ten minutes.

A spin-off from the main festival offered audiences a chance to see eight of the year's award winners, restaged at the plush Madinat theatre. The programme of entertaining and thought-provoking pieces highlighted the challenges the form presents for writers, directors and actors, and the creative spark required to excel in this medium.

The material has to make a swift impact, characters must be concisely defined and dilemmas clearly communicated. A satisfying pay-off is also desirable, though as this showing revealed, conclusions are somewhat elastic if some extended ad-libbing in character is necessary to cover a scene change.

For seven of the eight presentations a strong cast of just four actors played multiple roles. With minimal staging and straightforward costume, bar Elizabethan dress for the comic rewrite of *Romeo and Juliet*, the focus was on the ideas and the performances. These were my personal highlights.

Social media – aka the new lipstick on your collar for the unfaithful – was explored in *Tagged*, the comic opener written by Russell Bell. This worked for me on two levels. The characters and their relationships to each other were a tad overblown but underneath the laughter the play posed pressing questions about privacy, highlighting what we might be losing in an age where snapshots of our lives can be documented and put online by others.

To write a short play that is both funny and moving is a tall order but Jane Miller's, *Perfect Stillness* achieved that with a simple but clever idea. A husband writing a eulogy for his wife is chided by the deceased for his lack of honesty about their relationship. Two finely judged performances by the leads presented a more affecting reality. The ending invited us to ponder on whether the truth can ever be a welcome guest at a funeral.

The black comedy, *Last Drinks* introduced a deliciously odd pair with a curious synergy. Ben was determined to die but every attempt to commit suicide ended in failure, whilst Mel, in full bridal regalia attempted to drown her sorrows after her umpteenth potential husband expired before he could make it up the aisle. Over drinks they shared their pain, discovering they were made for each other – just before the final, laughable catastrophe.

The dramatic tensions of a love triangle had already earned *Somewhere between the Sky and the Sea*, by Alex Broun, a string of awards in previous festivals around the world. A composer that cannot choose between the two women in his life – the poetic sky and sea of the title – does not sound like a sympathetic character. The writing and the performances turned this notion on its head, and the beautifully conceived asides to the audience added layers of complexity to this conundrum.

A twist in the tale, or maybe that should be "tail" was brilliantly set up in *No. 22*. A group of captives in orange jumpsuits awaited their fate. Some of their number had already been taken and water torture was involved. In an atmosphere of grim humour, bad temper and out and out terror, the unfortunates displayed completely human responses. Until we realised they were not human, but a menu option. For me, the play should have ended at that very satisfying point.

Presented by Third Half Theatre the final presentation, *Tréteau* put the actor's craft in the frame. This was a tour de force performed by seven actors, with all the fast-paced action occurring within a tightly defined white box. Was that a Peter Brook reference? Everything was meaningful in this magic show where epic landscapes and mythical quests were conjured through a combination of physical theatre, mime, and heightened language. It was colourful, random, hard to comprehend at times, but thrilling to watch. Theatre as Jackson Pollock might have conceived it.

17

A Guest for Ramadan

An American fast food chain had been announcing its imminent arrival on giant hoardings for months. I was grateful that it waited till we were out of the country to finally open its doors to an eager crowd.

Sadly, this eyesore occupies a prime location at the entrance to Dubai Mall and within sight of the famous dancing fountains. With so many better and more comfortable dining options close by it was astonishing to see a long line queueing for a burger, hot dog and fries at all hours of the day and night. Change, if only for a month, was on the horizon and I was looking forward to my first Ramadan in Dubai.

Experiencing the Holy Month offered an opportunity to be better informed about the local culture and customs associated with this special time in the Islamic year.

Ramadan is one of the five pillars of Islam which all Muslims are expected to follow. The other four are Faith *(Shahadah)*, Prayer *(Salah)*, Charitable Giving *(Zakah)*, and the Pilgrimage to Mecca *(Hajj)*.

For Muslims, Ramadan involves a daily fast from sunrise to sunset. During the Holy Month, most restaurants and cafés were closed during the day, opening in the evening for the Iftar meal that breaks the fast. Some remain open till the small hours to offer

Suhour, the food eaten before the fast begins again at sunrise. Those that do stay open during the day serve discreetly, with blinds drawn in consideration and respect for those who are fasting. Eating, drinking, chewing gum and smoking in public is illegal during this time.

The fast is traditionally broken with dates and water but is more festive during the evening when friends and family or business colleagues come together for prayers and a larger meal.

As Ramadan is a time for reflection, self-improvement and charitable giving, the local media was full of ideas for ways that non-Muslim expats could feel engaged with their new locality during this time.

Sponsored by charities, companies, or individuals, mosques offer free Iftar meals to the less privileged members of society, whether they are Muslim or not.

At the other end of the spectrum many of the smart hotels put up special Iftar tents where customers pay for a feast. These ranged from new twists on Emirati specialties to just about every world cuisine imaginable. I spotted a listing for a Peruvian buffet and another venue focused on Cajun and Creole dishes. Yet another was staging its celebrations on Dubai's only revolving rooftop dining area.

Suggestions on what to wear to an Iftar, Ramadan hamper gift ideas and even Ramadan apps, indicated that much like Christmas, commercial imperatives, not to mention the convenience of the latest technology, had been woven into the fabric of Dubai's Ramadan celebrations. Useful perhaps for many of Dubai's residents, is the app calculating the percentage of total wealth that should be given to charity. Less fancy, but practical is the one linked to GPS, advising travellers on the correct prayer times across international time zones.

The etiquette for non-Muslim residents during Ramadan is mostly common sense and to do with behaving in a respectful way in public. Non-fasting drivers were advised to avoid the hours between 4pm and 7pm when roads were jammed with those rushing home to break their fast. It's easy to understand how concentration could be impaired for lack of food and water.

I had been invited to a hotel Iftar celebration and was looking forward to taking in the culinary atmosphere of Ramadan for the first time. To witness a buzzing metropolis move a little more slowly and traditionally would be a privilege.

18

Open Door for Iftar

You don't have to be in Dubai for long to notice that the expat communities vastly outnumber the local Emirati population. When we lived there, a BBC radio report indicated the ratio was one in nine. The cultural mix from around the world is rich and diverse but perhaps because of that, aside from the very obvious social protocols, the actual customs and religious traditions of the UAE are not always obvious.

The Sheikh Mohammed Centre for Cultural Understanding (SMCCU), established in 1998 helps to fill that gap, and address questions foreigners may have through a series of year-round educational programmes. Every evening during Ramadan, the Centre welcomes visitors and residents to an Iftar feast. Learning a little more about Islamic traditions by sharing the dishes typically eaten to break the fast is a charming concept, and the volunteers who host these evenings go out of their way to make this a special experience, as we discovered when we took up the invitation to learn more about the Holy Month.

Aside from trying a wonderful array of local food in an atmospheric and historic part of town, the evening also featured a visit to the nearby mosque during prayer time. Our hosts included a group of impressive young male and female Emirati volunteers who were keen that the assembled guests should have opportunities to ask them questions after the meal.

The food was laid out, buffet-style on a mat in the centre of the hall and once the fast had been broken with water, dates and Arabic coffee, the dishes were explained and we all helped ourselves, several times. There must have been at least a hundred guests for the meal but it was one of the most civilised buffets I've been to anywhere.

Many of the dishes were understandably very filling and this is a selection of the food and drink we enjoyed.

Arabic coffee, served at the start of the meal, is a drink of hospitality, a blend of lightly roasted Arabic beans, cardamom and saffron which is ground and boiled. The coffee is strained and served hot in small cups.

Machboos, a rice dish similar to biryani. The rice is seasoned and spiced with whole cardamom, cloves, cinnamon, and dried lemon. Yellow raisins and lentils are added and the dish is garnished with hard-boiled eggs.

Saloona, an Emirati stew of vegetables with lamb or chicken.

Fareeth, explained as Emirati lasagne, comprises thick layers of bread, covered with a stew of spiced meat and vegetables, braised until soft and tender.

Harees, a thick, savoury porridge made of wheat, meat and butter.

Ligamat, the Emirati version of doughnuts, served with lashings of date syrup.

Umali, a kind of creamy bread and butter pudding decorated with pistachio nuts and raisins.

Mahalabia, a sweet, set milk custard, flavoured with coconut.

Ramadan is a special time of year. Self-imposed deprivation encourages those who fast to face their weaknesses, admit their faults, and strive for self-improvement. One of the delights of this evening was how this and much else about the culture was explained with humour and humanity. One of the volunteers explained that she had stayed in bed till 1pm that day to make the fast easier and was finding it hard to fight her tendency to be lazy. Another said she recognised how she needed to control her temper because fasting made her more irritable than usual, particularly towards her siblings.

The spokesman for the group of volunteers could easily have had a career in comedy. He was hilarious, particularly on his experience of the western world's misconceptions of Arab culture. He quipped about the stereotypical response that he must be rich, have several wives and own an oil well. He was quite good on the worst assumptions too, particularly terrorism, and I wondered if he had taken lessons in delivery and attitude from the Jewish comedian, Jackie Mason. The punchlines were as profound as they were amusing and there was a genuine warmth and empathy to his riff on the affinities between religions and the respect he had for faith in general.

The questions were a little tame and even though the hosts said we could ask anything, it felt a little rude to be too provocative. I would have liked to have asked if the influences from all the diverse cultures in Dubai ever cause conflict for Emirati teenagers and their families. Do the young ever rebel and try to push the boundaries? Probably not, judging from the question on dating, which revealed a controlled and supervised pattern in which the words, "suitable," "approval," "engagement" and "dowry" were emphasised. There was no casual, experimental, or risky dating for these young people.

The issue of clothing did come up and one of the younger women said that no one forced her to wear the *abaya*. She wanted to wear Emirati national dress and she wore hers with pride. Male Emiratis wear the long white tunic known as the *kandura*. Someone asked her what she thought about visitors to her country that dress immodestly. Without hesitation she replied, 'Nothing at all, it is their choice.'

Such a non-judgemental attitude has to be admired when so many westerners take the view that women who cover up for cultural and religious reasons must, by implication, be oppressed.

19

A Brolly for All Seasons

As the temperatures in a Dubai summer regularly exceed 40°C I had to take a bit more care before casually stepping outside. Being outdoors for any length of time risked heat stroke for someone not used to it.

When I arrived in February ample supplies of high protection sun screen seemed to suffice, but I soon added a cheeky straw sun hat to the armoury. An oversized umbrella-cum-parasol in summer-bright turquoise was also put into service. It smacked of 19th century genteel but needs must.

I found it, hanging with its lime green companions in a Japanese novelty shop modelled on Poundland. A useful item at a bargain price was a rare find in Dubai Mall and it was proving its worth as my constant companion. One morning it even shielded me from attack by an aggressive crow.

The sober black collapsible version, my protector against the Yorkshire rain, had been relegated to the back of the cupboard. Damaged by one of those sudden Harrogate gusts but still functioning, this faithful friend made a brief re-appearance during a recent trip back to the UK, where downpours regularly interrupted play.

Using an umbrella for sun protection was a strategy the less hardy expats employed to cope with the soaring daytime temperatures. Summer also brought rising levels of humidity after dark and adaptation to these conditions brought with it some interesting contrasts.

I no longer woke up and looked out of the window to find out what the weather was like. There were no surprises and little variation. It was either boiling hot, even hotter than the hottest day on record, or hot with reduced visibility, due to a sandstorm.

I dressed with a certain confidence in the morning, safe in the knowledge that conditions would not change half way through the day rendering my outfit totally inappropriate.

Air-conditioning was a glorious relief from the heat but could be aggressively effective. The mall was not just for shopping, it was a comfort stop. Stay too long though, and you might need to head for the door in order to warm up. Sensible friends of mine carried a light cardi in their bag for just these moments.

Stepping from an air-conditioned car or apartment into an evening of high humidity was like being pushed towards an open oven door and a nightmare for those who wear glasses. I'd lost count of the amount of times I made an unsophisticated entrance into the lobby of a smart hotel with both lenses completely steamed up.

The glorious feeling of swimming in an outdoor pool at 10pm, when the air temperature was still in the 30s, or relaxing on a sun lounger under the night sky, was a new and gorgeous indulgence.

For the first time ever, I paid l attention to the use-by dates on food stuffs. Milk went off as the clock struck midnight on the date shown on the carton. Every time. It was a hard habit to break but I'd finally stopped overstocking the fridge. Daily shopping for fresh food you were going to eat in the next 24-48 hours was the way to go to avoid waste. Most foods had already been flown in from a long distance before going on sale, so had a short shelf life.

Accepting that it was too hot to enjoy eating al fresco was a tough one, as any Brit can appreciate and I no longer minded that hot water also came out of the cold tap. I was just grateful it was wet.

Driving trumped walking as the sensible option from May to October. Even walking a short distance in plus 40°C heat was deceptively hard going, as I had found out to my cost.

20

Thai Curry with Mona Lisa on the Side

It started out innocently enough. That fancy you get for something you've eaten before that really hits the spot if it's done right. Every cuisine we were used to finding in the UK was available in Dubai and I had been on a quest to track down a dish I knew was out there. The Thai green chicken curry of my dreams.

For me it would be freshly prepared, fragrant with lemongrass, kaffir lime leaves and galangal. A good chilli hit and a thin, but creamy and slightly sweet coconut milk sauce. Sections of baby aubergines bobbing on the surface, juicy pieces of chicken below and slivers of red chilli and lime leaf clinging to every spoonful. The authentic splash of salty fish sauce that brings all the sweet, sour, and spicy elements of the dish together had to be present too.

It shouldn't be that hard to find in a city with so many eating opportunities. My copy of Time Out Dubai listed nine Thai restaurants and that was a small sample. I'd tried five and only one of those appeared in the magazine's listing. I'd listened to recommendations and tried places that should be able to deliver the goods. Disappointment every time. So when I got a text from two different contacts suggesting I try a restaurant called *Smiling BKK,* I paid attention.

The website looked scary. Aside from the graphics, the menu selection at the bottom suggested that when they got bored with the run of the mill Thai stuff, they took liberties with spaghetti. Don't judge. Let's eat. Then judge.

This place needed to come with a warning. The interior resembled a confused and troubled teenager's bedroom. Identity crisis was writ large in the black curtains, and the highly varnished tables were giving off an aroma that could be mind-altering. That thought quickly evaporated because sensory overload kicked in from the multitude of coloured ceiling lights, two screens simultaneously showing American music videos, and the cardboard cut-outs of celebrities and dead Hollywood stars, randomly positioned around the room.

I was little unnerved by the life-size Justin Bieber that appeared to be giving me the eye as Michelle Obama looked on approvingly. It was hard to concentrate on the menu when Mickey Mouse hovered overhead and Austin Powers struck a pose close by, alongside a grinning and moustached Mona Lisa.

There was a toy gun on our table. When we were ready to order we were told to fire the gun and a waiter in a diamante baseball cap would come running. It all added up to a restaurant with the ambience of a David Lynch film. Maybe at the stroke of midnight a dwarf would emerge from the kitchen singing a Roy Orbison song backwards? I'd heard that this place attempted to recreate the atmosphere of a typical café in Bangkok. I have been to Bangkok and thankfully never encountered anything like this.

It took us ages to order because of all the distractions, plus every dish was irritatingly subtitled as a movie or pop song. In the teeth of all this nonsense I did notice some good-looking food arriving at nearby tables and other diners seemed to be tucking in, oblivious to the peculiar surroundings. Either they had been here before, so they were over the gimmicks, or the effects of the varnish had kicked in.

Someone in the kitchen was doing quite a bit right, though. My green chicken curry came close to perfection. The pea aubergines were a pleasing addition to the texture and authenticity and the base sauce had all the zing of the fresh herbs and citrus I was looking for. The fish sauce was missing though, so that extra layer of complexity wasn't quite there, but this was the best of its kind I'd had to date.

The prawn Tom Yum soup suffered from too much lime juice. We remedied this at the table with a spoonful of the curry sauce which softened the acidity but it too could have done with a spoonful of fish sauce for that authentic tang. The Pad Thai noodles had the fiery taste of the hot wok which I love and was served in an appetising mound, with a good helping of fresh beansprouts and crushed peanuts for added crunch. It was hard to resist and several helpings later, I knew why. It was extremely sweet. Not too much palm sugar for me but I suspect it would be for some.

The order also included a large bottle of sparkling water and a dish of steamed rice. For the total bill to come to only 125 dirhams, (just over £20) for two made this a surreal restaurant experience in itself. No wonder they said customers leave with a smile. It's either that or the varnish.

21

Letter from Lebanon

There is one call from home that every expat dreads. The one that comes without warning to tell you that a close relative is seriously ill and you need to come home. Fast. We had been in Dubai for just over three months when I received that call. My mother had been admitted to hospital in London with a catastrophic stroke. I was told she was conscious and breathing by herself and I knew she would be terrified. Fatal strokes run in our family. I caught the next available flight home. Despite the initial hopeful signs, her condition gradually deteriorated and she died a week later.

Mum had taken our move to Dubai in her stride, thanks to an advertising campaign. On television, twice nightly in the lead-up to our departure, exciting marketing shots of the city's landmarks and attractions put the right ideas about the place firmly in her mind. She was a Jewish mother and she worried about me going to the Middle East as only a Jewish mother can. I could get away with going to Dubai once she had glimpsed the appeal, but other places in the Middle East would trigger a red alert in her mind. Beirut was one. To my mother, Beirut was synonymous with conflict, danger, kidnapping and Hezbollah.

Weeks after my mother's funeral we visited Lebanon. I was missing her terribly and imagining how she would have tutted and complained to her friends about the location. 'Beirut, she goes! Only my daughter would choose Beirut!'

I wrote this letter home, wishing my mother could read it but at the same time knowing she never would.

I can still hear the worry in your voice, echoing in my head from several months ago when I first dropped Beirut into the conversation. Well, Mum, I went, I survived and I am back, safe and sound. I would have rung you by now to tell you all about it but since we can't have that kind of conversation any more I have written down what I would have told you about this trip.

No doubt about it, landing in Beirut after several months of life in Dubai was like stepping back into the real world from a Disney animation. It felt raw and chaotic after Dubai's ordered, manufactured facades, squeaky clean pavements and convenient living. Beirut might be rough and ready but it's also a city stuffed full of archaeological treasures, and it did its best to make us feel welcome and safe.

Shiny new apartment blocks have been plonked, higgledy-piggledy in and around dilapidated and damaged older buildings, many visibly pockmarked with bullets from the civil war and more recent bombardment.

In the central areas that were completely destroyed the rebuilding was better planned. I spent a morning strolling around the smart shops in the Beirut Souks, an attractive, contemporary interpretation of an outdoor Arab-style shopping market. After the usual indoor malls it made a pleasant change to be meandering in and out of the new walkways and wider avenues in the Mediterranean sunshine.

Lebanon is much more liberal than the UAE in terms of clothing and lifestyle. Muslim women are more individually dressed and wear colourful headscarves, mostly with western clothes. We arrived in Beirut during Eid, the festival that marks the end of Ramadan, so families and young adults were out in large numbers to enjoy the live music, street food, and the craft market near our hotel. Beirut TV was there too, with a glamorous young presenter covering live cooking demonstrations and interviewing stallholders.

One night we ate at one of the seafood restaurants on the Corniche, the famous beach front promenade, full of bars and smart venues that cemented Beirut's reputation in the 1960s as the Paris of the Middle East. Looking out across the sea to Mount Lebanon in the distance it was easy to imagine film stars like Omar Sharif and other rich and famous personalities sailing in on their yachts for some indulgent downtime. Mum, I remember you always liked Omar Sharif, especially in the film *Funny Girl* with Barbra Streisand. You thought he was dishy, didn't you?

We were grateful to be able to walk off our huge dinner with a stroll along the Corniche. We weren't expecting the restaurant to supply a complimentary platter of fruit, and dessert pots of chocolate, jelly and fragrant Lebanese cream pudding, but it was gratefully received.

Parts of Beirut were harder to explore on foot. In some areas, pedestrians were forced to walk in the road as so many cars were parked haphazardly on the pavement. Another problem was the increasing piles of uncollected rubbish blocking the footpaths. On the first night we joked that the binmen must be due the next morning, but it seemed we had stumbled on an unfolding crisis.

The authorities had failed to renew the contract for waste collection so the service was no longer operating, with alarming consequences. After a couple of days a toxic white powder was thrown over the stinking and growing heap. We concluded it must have been rat poison. As we negotiated our way around the mountain of waste, a car pulled up beside us. With windows wound down, the handsome young driver pointed to the eyesore. 'Welcome to Lebanon. *This* is Lebanon.' What a shame the obvious army presence around the city couldn't step in to save this young man's embarrassment and protect the population from a health hazard, and what would sadly become a metaphor for Lebanon's future. Who could have predicted how, in just five or six years Lebanon's economic fortunes would plummet, dragging the country and its long-suffering population into the worst financial and political crisis since the 1800s?

On our visit, before a scarcity of fuel and money would put them out of business, taxi drivers constantly cruised the streets on the hunt for weary pedestrians. A Lebanese colleague of Tim's warned us that these unregulated drivers were crooks but our experience didn't bear this out. With no meters, in theory they could charge what they thought they could get away with. Ours took us where we wanted to go, gave us a mini guided tour to various landmarks on the way, and then invited us to pay what we wanted. He appeared content with the amount of money we gave him.

Yes, we probably overpaid but no one was going to get rich from us paying the equivalent of eight pounds instead of five.

We hired an official driver to take us to significant sites outside Beirut, so we got to see a little more of Lebanon during our stay. We went to the mountain village of Harissa to take in the view of Beirut from a Catholic pilgrimage site and then on to Byblos, said to be one of the oldest cities in the world. The archaeological excavation site wouldn't have been your thing at all Mum, but I enjoyed it. The weather was just so gorgeous, it was great to be out in it and taking in the beautiful views. Later on we went for a walk around the nearby shop and restaurant complex. The majority of shops were selling jewellery and sandals and I kept imagining you picking things up and bargaining over something that you found irresistible. You wouldn't have come back empty-handed as I did, that's for sure.

Tim wanted to see the amazing rock formations in the Jeita Grotto. I wasn't prepared for the cable car journey to be an intrinsic part of this experience but I got through it with eyes closed. There was a boat trip on the subterranean lake included as well and that was quite relaxing, but a bit eerie.

One afternoon we ducked into the Saint George Greek Orthodox Cathedral and discovered there was a museum in the crypt with some surprising exhibits. The cathedral was damaged and then vandalised during the civil war but before it was restored, archaeologists uncovered layers of mosaics, burial places and artefacts from the Hellenistic, Roman, Byzantine, Medieval and Ottoman eras. I can see you yawning at this information but even you would have marvelled at the jewellery on display. Tiny stone necklaces and even a tiara! Best of all, did you know the Ottomans wore rings on their toes?

Well I guess that's all for now, Mum. You are in my mind all the time and I'm missing your responses to my adventures so much.

22

Jordan's Hidden Wonders

'You are welcome.' Such a simple phrase, usually just a reflex response to thanks, if used at all. It took a journey to Jordan for me to appreciate the real meaning of these words when spoken by a Jordanian. Everywhere we went, locals seemed genuinely delighted to see visitors and this oft repeated greeting was their way of communicating their pleasure.

Strolling past a café or a barber shop in the small town of Wadi Musa was enough to bring forth smiling locals, keen to impart these generous sentiments. We were routinely welcomed into taxis, to breakfast and re-welcomed on return to our hotel after a day out. Even the male housekeeper that cleaned our room deemed our presence warranted his personal salutation and a broad smile.

Despite the attraction of the ancient city of Petra, the town of Wadi Musa did not appear to be particularly prosperous. We had arrived at the hottest time of year when visitor numbers were low. Several hotels had closed, some for good we heard. The town's economy relies on tourism, so the less popular summer months were always a challenging period for local people. The government imposes high rates of tax on earnings from tourism and prices in and around the Petra site certainly seemed to reflect this.

All the taxi drivers made a point of asking about outward flight times in the hope of securing a lucrative fare to Amman airport, a three-hour drive away. Most were willing to undercut whatever price had been quoted by someone else. We were soon adopted by a particularly assertive but helpful taxi driver who made up his mind he would take us everywhere we needed to go, at all times. Resistance was useless but it was thanks to him that we made the very sensible decision to explore the Petra site at 6.30am before the heat of the day made walking around really uncomfortable.

I knew virtually nothing about Petra before this trip but now I know that it was built by the Nabataeans who ruled Jordan from the 3rd century B.C. until the 1st century A.D. They became wealthy spice traders and absorbed the influences of other cultures, evident in the architectural features at Petra, which was once a busy capital city. When the civilisation went into decline, Petra was abandoned and lost to the world, until a Swiss traveller rediscovered the ruins in 1812. In 1989, Hollywood came to Jordan to film an *Indiana Jones* blockbuster at the site. In 2007 Petra was named as one of the Seven New Wonders of the World.

We checked into our hotel in time to join a candlelit walk to the Treasury, the most impressive and complete monument on the site. After the long walk through a narrow gorge a section of a ghostly façade, illuminated by flickering candlelight came into view. A musical performance on an early version of the guitar was laid on, and while we sat sipping our sweet black tea we could gaze in wonder at the whole and marvel how it had all been carved from a single piece of stone. It is so magnificently intact that the night time atmosphere made it seem like a trick, an illusion. It is mesmerising and despite the long trek to get there all I could think about was coming back to fully appreciate the pink stone of the Rose City in daylight, hence the decision, after a day of rest, to return at 6.30am.

On the way back a distant rat-a-tat-tat kept interrupting the peace. It sounded like gun fire. Was Jordan at war or could it be coming from the Israeli border? It wasn't until the next day that we found out that it was a wedding party. Guns are routinely fired into the air by way of celebration within these communities. It happened the next night too and this time the friendly waiters at a nearby hotel, who knew the happy couple, explained that there was no imminent danger.

Visiting Petra, as we observed on the candlelit walk, is not for the faint-hearted. The mile-long walk through the Siq is over uneven ground and quite hard to negotiate in semi-light. Returning, when I could see where I was going more clearly, made me realise that without Tim to hold on to I could have easily taken a tumble.

The Treasury is even more dramatic in daylight as all the detail of the dusky pink exterior is revealed. Walking on from there we passed high points of religious significance with spectacular views, rows of tombs and temples with intricate carvings, the remains of a magnificent amphitheatre and a colonnaded street which was once the main thoroughfare. I declined to tackle the eight hundred steps cut into a mountain, leading to the Monastery and the pinnacle of the Petra site, but Tim bravely ascended on a donkey. Even the poor animal could only go so far and Tim wisely stopped short of the full climb. The view and the Monastery must be just as impressive from five hundred steps.

All around the Petra site rickety souvenir stalls and cafés run by locals were helping overheated tourists take a break and catch their breath. I had heard that the author of the memoir, *Married to a Bedouin* ran one of the souvenir stalls.

We soon spotted a board advertising her book and whilst we were browsing, Marguerite van Geldermalsen, the writer in question, introduced herself. She kindly signed my copy and I also purchased a grossly overpriced hand-made silver necklace from her. I couldn't resist when she told me the design was based on one of the decorative features of the Treasury. Worth it for a lasting memento of a visit to Petra. Her book left me with so many questions. As she tells it, she went from life as a single Western woman, to living in a cave with a Bedouin husband without the slightest anxiety. I find it hard to believe the adjustment was quite as easy as described and that there was nothing she missed about her own culture and background.

The walk back is uphill and in daytime the last part of the route is in full sun. The Bedouins offering bumpy rides in horse-drawn buggies can virtually name their price – ours even took Visa. In fact this proved a little more complicated than envisaged when we climbed in, as the credit card facility relied on the driver's mates near the visitor centre to help out.

So what did we eat? Jordan's food has much in common with other Middle Eastern countries. Appetisers are the mezze dishes, identical to those we have had in Lebanon and Dubai – piles of Arabic flatbread, served with dishes of hummus, tabbouleh, moutabal, which is a smooth aubergine and garlic dip, and an Arabic salad of diced cucumber and tomato.

A colleague of Tim's alerted us to try the traditional Bedouin specialities, including *Mansaf*, Jordan's national dish. Our hotel offered a typical Bedouin dinner option, served in a tent, with the main courses cooked, desert-style, in underground ovens and *Mansaf* was on the menu. This version of lamb on the bone, slow cooked in fermented yoghurt until meltingly tender was exceptionally good. The dish, served with rice was enclosed in Arabic bread which had a slight crispness to it from the oven. I was less keen on the accompanying warm yoghurt sauce. Freshly chopped mint stirred through might have worked in its favour but the dish was very tasty without the sauce.

Tim tried *Mandi,* a delicious roasted chicken dish served on top of lightly spiced rice with sweet carrots. Another recommendation which we didn't try on this trip is *Maklouba,* which means upside down. Meat, rice and vegetables, arranged in layers in a deep pot are cooked slowly. Before serving the pot is upended so all the meaty juices flavour the rice and vegetables. There's always next time.

23

Take Me Back to the China Sea

I'd been fancying a Chinese meal ever since Tim came back raving about a particular dish on offer at Dubai's *China Sea* restaurant. He'd been promising to take me there to share the joy.

The stars aligned and one evening we headed for this beacon of flashing red and gold kitsch, illuminating the whole street. Every Chinese adornment, from fringed and bobbing lanterns to rampant mythical beasts, and then some, was on show at this Dubai institution.

I'd recently made a brief trip to *Dragon Mart*, a terrifyingly huge shopping complex, offering every conceivable product created and manufactured in China. A considerable proportion of these wares had found a home at *China Sea*. Come sundown the building's glow attracted hordes of hungry customers in, like proverbial moths to a flame.

The menu was book-sized and in any other setting this would be a worrying sign, but from our table I could see the kitchen was alive with cooking to order action and the sound of utensils hitting hot woks was audible. A team of waitresses in jade green uniforms were wheeling trolleys of freshly prepared individual dishes to their destinations, carefully ticking the items off a handwritten list at the table, on delivery.

All nationalities were tucking in. A large party of Chinese diners had just finished their meal and seemed to be creating a noisy kerfuffle near the kitchen. It was hard to know if a couple of the group were just exhibiting high spirits or about to hit each other. It sounded, and certainly looked like a close run thing at one point, but when the kitchen staff appeared the potential trouble evaporated and the crowd dispersed.

Meanwhile the plates moving past our table looked so appetising and with so many of the dishes on the menu also illustrated, it was time to be experimental. A display area of chilled fresh ingredients and prepped plates, plus a tank of live fish, offered additional off-menu choices for the adventurous diner.

"Deep-fried eggplant shrimps in sauce," said the menu. It might even have said, "special sauce." If it didn't it most definitely should. I love eggplant, or aubergine, as I know it. Shrimps are usually what Brits understand as prawns. Never had them together until this dish. I had been deprived.

On the plate were at least two aubergines, each cut into thick rounds so they remained attached but separated, like a fan. A plump prawn was sandwiched between each slice. It came to the table in an attractive, neat arrangement, the whole having been plunged into boiling oil and covered in the promised sauce. The inside of the aubergine was juicy and unctuous in the eating, yet retained some bite. The purple black skin had a sweet crunch. A brown, gloopy, savoury/sweet liquid oozed across the whole plate. Everything about this was wrong but it was utterly delicious.

I attracted the attention of our waitress before I realised that her English was limited, and my question about how the dish was made was too subtle. Sometimes it is best not to ask but I ploughed on, stupidly pointing at the plate of aubergine which seemed to delight her. With a huge smile she simply said, 'Yes!' Just in time, we managed to let her know that we definitely didn't need to order a second plate of it. That would have been ridiculous.

Those who love tofu insist on extolling its virtues. They say things like: You can do so many things with it. OK. How many of those are edible? Or: It soaks up any other flavour you put with it. How is this a selling point? It is still tofu. Flavoured tofu. Finally, and somewhat desperately in my view: It is SO good for you. The texture varies from silken to firm, which to a non-tofu fan is doublespeak for the viler the texture, the more good it is doing you. Well I take it all back. Tofu isn't, as I previously believed, the food of the devil.

The dish I had come for was a noodle salad with a punchy chilli oil dressing and fresh coriander. It was waiting for me in the chiller. The noodles were crafted from tofu, but you would never know it, which to a tofu hater and noodle lover is great news. I could have eaten a whole bowl of this salad and been happy with just that. Maybe.

On this occasion we also ordered a plate of mixed stir-fried green vegetables, dressed with dried chillies, barbecued crispy duck with pancakes and a large plate of fried rice with mixed seafood. The duck was a dish of two halves. First, a plate of skin and bones, the idea being to chew on these and suck all the meaty flavour from them before the slices of prime duck meat arrived.

We were less impressed with the bony, chewy bits but felt this was a small gripe in light of the whole experience.

The China Sea Customer Feedback Questionnaire is a thing of remarkable detail. Anything less than complete customer satisfaction is not an option. We were invited to compliment or complain on the speed of dish delivery, taste, waitress service and single out the best and worst dishes. Boxes had to be ticked in all categories: Very Fast, Very Slowly, Nice, Just So So, Insipid, Very Good, Very Bad and curiously, More Oil. The staff members carefully studied our response sheet.

The one question not fully explored on the form is value for money, which is outstanding. The equivalent of just £15 each for all that food and fun. Priceless.

24

Mixed Media

Is it a play or is it a film? That is the question. Or certainly that was the one I was asking as we took our seats at Dubai's Courtyard Playhouse.

We were here for a National Theatre Live screening of *The Audience*, Peter Morgan's award-winning play starring theatrical royalty, Dame Helen Mirren. I'd always wondered whether seeing a broadcast of a play on a cinema screen counts as a true theatrical experience but given that London's theatre scene was out of reach, this seemed a good moment to find out how it all worked.

The filmed performance featured the original cast and also included a post-show discussion between Dame Helen and director Stephen Daldry.

The venue was an intimate, refurbished performance space, with comfortable red velvet seats giving an appropriate sense of occasion. The broadcast in front of the original audience began before the houselights went down, so we saw the audience in their seats and later heard them respond with applause and laughter that we shared, but were not part of. The urge to clap a well-delivered speech, and especially when the actors took their bows was a reflex response but felt a little odd in the absence of the flesh and blood players.

The play invited us to eavesdrop on the famously private weekly conversations between the present Queen and the prime minister of the day. Through imagined, yet credible exchanges, Helen Mirren's brilliant and transformative performance as Queen Elizabeth II ran from her accession to the throne in 1952, through to more recent times.

Lightening changes of clothes and wigs, some cunningly magical, were remarkably effective and through the leading lady's nuanced performance and vocal dexterity we witnessed the young Elizabeth Windsor grow in confidence, acquiring the wit and wisdom her prime ministers would come to rely on as they and the monarchy were tested over six decades.

The narrative was not presented chronologically so the audience were kept in the dark as to who would appear next. A roll call of British political leaders featured Winston Churchill, John Major, Anthony Eden, David Cameron, Margaret Thatcher, Harold Wilson, Gordon Brown, and a cameo appearance by James Callaghan. Tony Blair was glossed over but written into the Broadway production, due to his popularity in the US. During the allotted twenty minute confessional each PM revealed their own human and political frailties, along with the issues of the day.

The mood was varied, as the script required much more of the actors than mere impersonation. Some of the most touching moments occurred when John Major, Gordon Brown and Harold Wilson voiced self-doubts. They received a sympathetic and understanding hearing, in between the gentle teasing on both sides that I would love to believe actually happened. The writer gave the Queen a razor sharp wit and Mirren's comic timing was spot on.

Like a silk thread woven into the play, Elizabeth's encounters with her younger self, kicking against her pre-determined destiny added an extra layer of complexity. There was a satisfying irony here, as in the later discussion Dame Helen revealed that before she read the script she too decided that she didn't want to play the Queen for a second time. Starring in the acclaimed film of the same name, also written by Peter Morgan, made her the obvious choice but for that reason she believed it was time to move on. Whatever doubts Dame Helen may have had soon evaporated when she realised the production and design team represented the cream of British theatre and she would be crazy to turn the opportunity down.

To make the NT Live experience satisfying, characters were often seen in close-up or from angles that wouldn't normally be possible. This illustrated both the advantages and the limitations of this hybrid. In the post-show interview Dame Helen explained that acting for a theatre audience and the camera simultaneously, is a skill she felt she hadn't yet perfected. There were moments when the camera seemed a fraction too close to work successfully for the film viewer, and for a second or two our favourite Dame seemed to teeter on the edge of panto. The fault of the medium, rather than the performer.

The odd misjudged camera angle far outweighed the pleasure of experiencing one of London's best theatre productions from a distant location.

25

Home to Sound and Fury

Returning to Dubai after a holiday made it seem less like a fantastic experiment and much more like real life. What caused this subtle shift in thinking? The occupants of the flat above ours and their home improvements mostly, but more of that later.

In the previous month we had enjoyed time with family and friends in Venice and the UK and also attended two wonderful celebrations. At a wedding in London and a birthday party in Denmark, we felt like VIPs. We were the interesting pair that live in Dubai and the guests that had covered more miles to be present than anyone else. Where we lived and what our life was like was a topic of interest to everyone we met. It had started to feel good to talk about it. We had positive things to say and we could answer most people's questions with first-hand experience and good humour.

Making the leap from the UK to Dubai had put ideas in our heads. Home was becoming an elastic concept. For the first part of our holiday we rented an apartment in Venice, away from the crowds. As soon as we had the keys we started to imagine ourselves living like Venetians on a permanent basis, picking up fruit and veg daily from that magnificent display by "our" bridge, and strolling to the nearest square for an early evening glass of wine and the delicious snacks that Italians always serve with alcohol.

We were in Venice as a family to see the international contemporary art exhibition, held every two years. Overall, the Venice Biennale, 2015 lacked the optimism and resonance of previous years but in a city that can never disappoint, we all found plenty to enjoy here, especially on the food front.

So on to the UK. This would feel like home, wouldn't it? Familiar yes, but this would be the last time I would have a reason to go up this particular path and ring the bell. The keys to Mum's house would soon be handed over to a new occupant and we were there to remove the contents and let go. For different reasons we had undergone much the same process when we left our former home in Harrogate after more than twenty years in residence.

Denmark gave us the Indian summer temperatures we didn't have in the UK and the time to enjoy a boat trip in the sunshine. End of season beauty, for this area would soon turn chilly, grey and wet. Having survived Dubai's ferocious summer heat we were already beginning to anticipate the journey back, hoping the more tolerable winter temperatures had started to kick in.

And so we returned to the Dubai bubble of wacky skylines and rampant consumerism, but something big and noisy had arrived unannounced, shattering the calm in our building.

Doors were open and strangers of all nationalities were introducing themselves to each other, holding their heads and pointing upwards. We were bonding over a common enemy. The cuckoo in the nest on the next floor was using a jack hammer to destroy a perfectly good, tiled floor. The drilling noise went on for hours, day after day. No explanation, no information.

It was a peculiar form of torture. When it started, every tooth in my head felt loose. I dropped objects and could not think straight. A screeching monster had taken over my tranquil haven and was forcing me out. There is nothing quite like a crisis to prompt defensive action in a Brit. This is my home if you don't mind! Not just my home, but also my workplace.

The other residents were equally aggrieved but lacked action. Leave it to me. Suddenly, I was everyone's representative on the topic of noise. The prestigious property management company that granted permission for the work to go ahead seemed to have overlooked their own rules on creating an unacceptable disturbance. Security was called and after much discussion and a demonstration of the said jack hammer in action, all work ceased.

The home improver knocked on our door and gave a weak apology. If ever there was an opportunity to give someone with little empathy some useful feedback it was at this point. I suggested the ways his interior design project could have been managed to avoid such universal unhappiness.

The next day negotiations between the owner, the contractor and myself began. After several days of respite, allowing everyone's hackles to subside, with my permission, the contractors were granted prescribed hours over one day to complete all the work. I made sure I was out for the majority of it and advised my neighbours to do the same.

Peace was eventually restored to the building but the disruption had introduced me to more residents in a few days than in the previous eight months. All it takes is a little local difficulty to feel right at home, wherever you are.

26

Working to Enhance My Experience

Refurbishment, fit out or maintenance works in Dubai's public areas invariably carry explanatory signage with the motto, *Working to Enhance Your Experience,* suggesting that the temporary inconvenience is for the greater good. This delightful phrase suggests that behind the hoardings, persons unseen are labouring night and day to get things back on track as soon as possible.

Whether this is actually true or not is questionable as alterations to existing premises could go on for months, with no discernible difference to the décor or layout on conclusion. Leaving that to one side, the sentiment resonated with me and was one I took to heart.

No one back in the UK had actually asked me what I did all day in Dubai. It was only the voice inside my head that stopped me in my tracks if a particularly lazy day was planned. It was all too easy to become indolent and frankly, spoilt in this environment. Dubai's expat community certainly had its fair share of over-indulged adults, happy to voice their first world problems without a trace of self–awareness. In the wild, and at a safe distance, this particular breed was fascinating to observe but liable to set your teeth on edge if encountered at close quarters. I lived in perpetual fear of turning into one of them.

For those of my friends and relatives that assumed I spent my time lunching, shopping and sipping cocktails, and for my own sanity, I noted down my recent activities.

Cinema. I'd heard an interview with the director of *Legend*, and was amazed to find that it was showing at the local multiplex. A film charting the rise and fall of the notorious Kray twins in 1960s London was akin to art house in Dubai. I was so keen to see this film after listening to the interview that I went by myself one afternoon while Tim was on a business trip to Saudi Arabia. I didn't know anyone else that would have been remotely interested in the subject matter, and it would have taken too long to explain. The film dug deep into the dysfunctional psychology of the Kray twins. Tom Hardy playing both roles was a neat trick to pull off and his performance was outstanding.

Desert safari. This was a trip to Dubai's Conservation Reserve organised specifically for our younger son's visit and one that appealed to me because it offered a trek to the desert in relative comfort, with no rufty, tufty dune bashing. It was well worth getting up at the crack of dawn to appreciate the beauty of the desert before the serious heat of the day. Our tour included a stop at the camel racetrack, breakfast at a Bedouin village, a Q&A with the village leader (no personal questions about family or wealth, please), an introduction to the protected gazelles and antelopes and the terrifying highlight – a camel ride. The collapse of the beast's legs as it lowered itself to the ground, thus allowing the rider to dismount, took me by surprise, but I survived.

Abu Dhabi. My first visit to the capital of the United Arab Emirates and a tour of the magnificent Sheikh Zayed Grand Mosque. The famed eighty-two white marble domes and the sheer scale of the site was impressive. I didn't expect to be so wowed by the stunning chandeliers in the prayer hall, or the contemporary beauty of the floral motif in the main courtyard created by British artist, Kevin Dean.

Brushing up my Shakespeare. I signed up for a six-week course led by a player from Shakespeare's Globe and National Theatre. A thoroughly enjoyable opportunity to experience the challenging techniques and exercises used by the UK's stage professionals. It was ironic that I'd come all the way to Dubai to reconnect with my drama student days in London half a lifetime ago, but maturity certainly helped to enhance this experience.

27

Pick and Mix Christmases

By any measure, Christmas 2020 was surely one of the weirdest. The politicians decided that all the restrictions on liberty we had endured from March to December could be relaxed during the holiday, to allow a limited number of family members to be together. At the last moment, and with evidence that a new variant of the coronavirus was taking hold, the scientists advised that different households should limit contact to Christmas Day only, and preferably avoid meeting at all. Retail, for the most part had moved online and for many it was a case of enduring Christmas, rather than indulging themselves in it. In the face of a virulent disease the whole festive 2020 UK shebang just didn't have the same sparkle.

I didn't expect our first Christmas in Dubai to add up to much either but I couldn't have been more wrong. Dubai, of all places got Christmas just about right, as I recall.

Black Friday, Cyber Monday and all the rest of the hideous panic buying that usually makes the countdown to December 25 a nightmare in the UK, did not happen there. It probably was happening at some level but that is my point. You did not have to take part in all that if like me, you hanker after a calmer lead up to the festive period.

In a country where Christmas is not a compulsory part of the cultural and religious landscape the preparations are in proportion. Everything required for a jingle bells celebration is certainly available, from real trees, to carol concerts, it's just not in your face, night and day for weeks in advance.

Don't get me wrong, I enjoy aspects of Christmas but I don't like what it has become in the UK. First off, it seems to start soon after the summer holiday season when the beach-ready features are repurposed for, "shaping up and slimming down to shine" articles in the magazines, and gaudy decorations line the aisles in the supermarkets.

There are endless debates on whether the high street and online retailers can expect a bumper Christmas, how much money will be made or not and the commercial wisdom of bringing the January sales forward to December whilst everyone is in spending mode. There is invariably an item that will famously not be available in the UK in time for Christmas morning and tales of disappointment or triumph associated with said item. Thanks to the BBC, I heard it all play out as per usual from Dubai. Here are some more UK Christmas "traditions" I could do without.

The way Christmas TV adverts, driven by large commercial organisations, are delivered and received as short films, worthy of serious discussion by intelligent people. They are trying to sell us stuff. Nothing more.

The sinking feeling that comes with placing an online festive gift order with a likely delivery date of January.

Queuing in the cold and dark to use a cash machine.

Clearing and defrosting the freezer in time to refill with enough food to feed the population of a small country.

Worrying about all the presents I haven't yet bought, whether the turkey I have ordered is too big/ too small/ and whether transport strikes or weather will stop our sons travelling from where they are, to wherever we are.

High street shopping when Wizard, Slade, Wham and Michael Bublé's Christmas songs are the soundtrack to every purchase.

In a city where shopping and spending is practically a national sport and glitter and sparkle are year-round necessities, Christmas is cut down to size. It was certainly outshone by early December's UAE National Day parade through the streets.

The musical procession went past our apartment and given the horror of the multiple terrorist attacks in Paris the previous month, it was heart-warming to see so many nationalities and cultures represented in the floats that made their way along Mohammad Bin Rashid Boulevard. Just flag waving and national pride? Yes, but the message on one banner was my takeaway. It simply read, *We All Smile in the Same Language.* A great motto for a Christmas cracker.

Before we arrived we speculated about what Christmas in Dubai might look like. Should we take the decorations with us? Surely not. Likewise, the oversized fake tree that came down from the loft every year? No, that would be silly too. Wise decisions. Without all the familiar festive paraphernalia to hand, it was so much easier to break away from convention and adopt a fresh approach.

The traditionalists and those with small children could find all they needed in Dubai to make the festive season bright –

including a white Christmas. One of the big department stores had added a snow machine to Santa's habitat, recreating the magic of Lapland.

Fake snow was easy to find but the odds remained resolutely stacked against impressing the adults with a half decent mince pie. I'd sampled examples at the most popular British expat haunts but soggy pastry and a lack of decent filling, of the right taste and consistency had been the norm. When I spotted mince pies amongst the very tempting cake display at our local independent deli, hope surged anew.

Unfortunately, the concept of pie had been interpreted literally and this one had a pastry lid so thick it needed a knife and fork to penetrate. The filling was an unsatisfying black paste with an overpowering flavour of cloves, possibly to compensate for the lack of brandy. Overall, it was a bit medicinal, which is not really what anyone wants from a mince pie.

A couple of supermarkets stocked mince pies with a long shelf life from the kitchens of Mr Kipling and Mr Lyons. The trusty M&S and Waitrose luxury versions weren't flown in, possibly because of their perishability and booze content. Shop bought mincemeat was tricky too. My search was long and involved fruitless conversations (pun intended), with confused shop assistants about the meaning of mincemeat in this context. Quite by chance I came upon two jars of the stuff sitting lonely amongst a random clutch of unrelated products in a small supermarket. By this time I had planned to make my own mincemeat anyway but the purchase felt sweet.

Back home in Harrogate, I could always rely on the town's famous craft bakery to supply the best mince pies on the planet but not this year. With none of the usual pre-Christmas panic I quite fancied the idea of calmly rolling out pastry in air-conditioned comfort, whilst listening to the radio. I should point out that there was a time, back in the 1980s when I experienced my first Christmas in Adelaide, in a flat with no air-conditioning. It involved roasting a duck in my underwear and I don't think it gets more stupidly British than that.

A few weeks before our first Christmas in Dubai we'd spent a weekend in Al Ain, one of the largest cities in the UAE, but with a much older and more traditional heritage than Dubai. There is a famous camel market there which turned out to be prophetic. I spotted a smallish decorative ceramic camel in the lobby of our hotel and so Colin, our Christmas camel was duly purchased, installed on a bench top, and decorated with festive red tinsel.

Candles, strategically placed baubles, and pretty fairy lights was enough, and the countdown was on until our sons arrived. Requests for chill-out time around the pool had been received and a favourite venue had been booked for Christmas lunch, so no final lists or battling the crowds for last minute food items. I missed the lovely smell of turkey stock permeating the house on Christmas Eve, though, which is why I went in a different direction the following year, when Christmas lunch was a home-cooked affair.

For our second Christmas a turkey from an organic farm, somewhere in Tipperary graced our table on the due date. As the song says, it's a long way to Tipperary, especially from Dubai, but such is the price us expats pay to recreate our traditions when abroad. If Yorkshire farmers could have supplied, my joy would have been complete, but I was grateful for what I could get, even if the price reflected the said turkey's first class journey.

The festive fowl was readily available in Dubai. You just needed to decide where you wanted it to originate from and how you wanted to receive it. Turkeys from Germany, Hungary and from unspecified, local locations were on offer. Some claimed to be organic, others had been sitting frozen in supermarket cabinets for months. The occasional fresh bird could appear unannounced on the poultry counters at any time of year and especially ahead of Thanksgiving.

Hundreds of lavish venues laid on what they believed to be a traditional Christmas meal. The Christmas lunch we'd experienced in a hotel close by was wonderful, the choice of dishes huge, but the traditional stuff wasn't the best thing on offer that day. The barbecued seafood and seared scallops were the better choices as the turkey lacked flavour and the accompaniments weren't quite right. Going out or cooking at home were not the only options, though. This was Dubai, after all.

You could opt to have your Christmas meal cooked and delivered on the day, with all the trimmings included. Adverts showing a golden bird, surrounded by crisp roast potatoes, lush green sprouts and shiny cranberries looked tempting enough. There was no shortage of businesses ready to make it happen for those that prized convenience over effort. I just didn't fancy handing the whole responsibility to someone else and then being disappointed when it failed to taste home-cooked and traditional. If I mucked up, then the buck stopped with me. I also needed to know where the bird had come from and if it had enjoyed a happy and stimulating life. The one we'd had at the hotel tasted as if it had died of boredom.

So it was a case of making shopping lists, digging out those tried and tested stuffing recipes once again and wondering if one of my offspring could slip a Christmas pudding in his hand luggage.

This was the one and only Christmas when the catering was actually in proportion to the number of diners at the table. I didn't have the fridge and freezer capacity to create a banquet in advance, or start hoarding as if food shortages were imminent. Plus, the oven in our apartment was smaller than the average British appliance and could therefore only accommodate a turkey of modest size. Pretty much everything prepared fresh on Christmas Eve would need to be consumed the next day, with only one meal of leftovers, max, not counting the stock that would be made from the turkey carcass after the main event. It would have been churlish not to as it had travelled all the way from Tipperary for our delight.

28

New Year, New View

The unplanned New Year's Eve fireworks in Dubai caught us all napping. From our balcony, on the most predictable evening of the year, we saw fire break out at the luxury hotel across the road and watched in horror as the flames rapidly moved up the exterior of a sixty-three-storey building. Had anyone else noticed what we could see?

In a matter of minutes news reports and alarming pictures of an escalating disaster had travelled across the globe. I have never been more grateful for mobile phone technology and social media. After an anxious wait we ascertained the whereabouts and safety of two friends who lived in the hotel's residential apartments, and were able to offer refuge to others who were evacuated from a nearby restaurant. As messages came in from friends and family worldwide we could reassure them that we were out of harm's way, though, yes, this *was* happening quite close to where we lived.

Unbelievably, come midnight the planned pyrotechnics went ahead, regardless of the smoke and nearby flames that threatened the Happy New Year messages lighting up the Burj Khalifa.

Black smoke was still billowing out from the hotel two days later and by then we learned that one friend had lost everything in the fire. Another was waiting to be allowed in to see if anything could be salvaged, as her apartment had been deluged by the automatic sprinkler system. Everyone we knew was safe but traumatised.

When the authorities decided that the area around the hotel was safe for pedestrians, the crowds returned. Before the fire, the cameras and selfie sticks were angled to take in the Burj Khalifa. In the days after the blaze, the tallest building in the world had competition. Bizarrely, tourists were more attracted to the opposite view and were using the exterior of a famously fire-damaged luxury hotel as a backdrop for their social media posts.

The fire made us think about what we would want to save, should we have to evacuate our building at any stage. In an emergency there is no time to gather your thoughts. It would be sensible in this unpredictable world to focus on the items that would be helpful in such a situation and leave them in a small bag close to the front door, just in case.

I promised my eldest son, who takes these things very seriously, that I would do this. I am quite a material girl and it was a surprise to me that I could be so practical. My choices would definitely make me feel better able to face the world if I had to abandon the comfort of home.

This was the list I came up with, bearing in mind I was not living in my home country and that I would probably be wearing the items of jewellery that mean the most to me.

- Passport, birth and marriage certificate
- Some cash
- Paper copies of credit and bank card details
- Basic set of toiletries and make-up

- Hairbrush
- Change of clothes
- Comfortable shoes
- Spare mobile phone
- Spare pair of glasses and sunglasses

What would you take?

29

On the Indian Food Trail

Dubai is overflowing with glitzy, expensive restaurants but there is another side to this food-loving city. Old Dubai is crammed with Indian street food sellers, artisan food producers, family–run restaurants and ethnic grocery stores, offering authentic regional specialities at bargain prices. We had made tentative inroads to this other world but knowing where to go and what to order required serious insider knowledge. Enter *Frying Pan Adventures,* a small, local tour company started and run by two food-loving sisters.

I found this enterprise on Twitter before we arrived in Dubai and made a mental note to check out one of their walking food tours. My first attempt at booking was unsuccessful. Their events are extremely popular and the available dates sell out fast because the tour groups have to be small in number for practical reasons. The street food businesses on the route get busier as the evening progresses. Managing a large group down a narrow side street, noisy thoroughfare and indeed, working kitchen could be problematic and frustrating for everyone. In a small group there were more opportunities to get to know others on the tour and to ask the organiser questions as you taste.

Our tour guide through the bustling Meena Bazaar was an enthusiastic and informative ambassador for Dubai's Indian food community. All the dishes we tried were seasoned with tasty titbits of Indian history, epic love stories, dashes of Sanskrit, and the food heritage and traditions associated with her own family.

The food of India is of course an enormous topic and the tastings over one evening could only be a small snapshot. I say small, but there was no shortage of food. Second and even third helpings of everything were on offer and by the end of the trail I was certainly very full.

The amount of fried food and sugar we consumed over four hours would have horrified the nutrition police, and whilst the majority of dishes were vegetarian it was surprising that the vegetables that take on Indian flavours so well were not in evidence at all. The inclusion of a little cauliflower, aubergine or spinach would certainly have provided balance in light of what was to come.

Towards the end of the evening the sweet versus savoury ratio went out of the window completely and for those without a super sweet tooth, digesting two rich desserts either side of a main course was challenging.

The dishes I really enjoyed were the savoury snacks or *chaat*. You could make a meal of these by themselves or just have one or two to whet your appetite for the main event.

At *Rangoli* restaurant we started with *pani puri*, a liquid-filled Indian fried dough ball filled with green gram sprouts, black chickpeas and potatoes. The *boondi* version is made out of fried gram flour, spicy chilli water and sweet date chutney. These have to be popped in the mouth whole as they are filled with liquid and the dough collapses in seconds. A dainty bite is not an option for this reason, which is why I ended up wearing my first *pani puri*.

Bhel puri is puffed rice with onions, raw mangoes, tomatoes, crushed puris, spices and deep-fried gram flour noodles called *sev*, the main ingredient of Bombay mix. This dish had texture and crunch and all the different ingredients looked really attractive on the plate.

Dahi batata puri was my favourite here. So many contrasts and tastes all in one mouthful! This fried dough ball was stuffed with potatoes, garlic, red chilli chutney, spicy chilli water, sweet date chutney, yogurt, powdered cumin and deep-fried gram flour noodles.

We stopped at the *Farisian Cafeteria* for a bag of potato *bhondas,* which had been dipped in a gram flour batter before frying, plus some onion samosas. A delicious spicy green chutney brought out the flavours of these beautifully.

The Sangeetha Restaurant let us into the kitchen where the chefs were preparing *dosas* and frying *puris*. We sat down to try their Mini Tiffin, a complete meal comprising a variety of different small dishes:

Masala dosa, a fermented rice and black gram lentil crepe, stuffed with mashed, curried potatoes.

Topi dosa, a hat shaped crisp crepe – pieces are broken off and dipped into coconut, coriander or mixed lentil chutney.

Mini idlis in sambar – steamed discs of fermented rice and split black lentil paste in a lentil stew.

Medu vada, a savoury doughnut made with black gram flour.

Rava upma, a semolina and split black lentil mash.

Pongal rice and green gram lentil mash, served with *sambar*.

The Mini Tiffin came with a dessert called *kesari*, a semolina-sugar-ghee *halwa* and a steaming hot cup of Madrasi filter coffee.

The flavours here were interesting, but not outstanding and everything, bar the *topi dosa* was the same soft texture. I have eaten *dosas* in Bradford and these were stuffed with potatoes too. I wondered why a less starchy vegetable filling wasn't used. It was all a bit too stodgy for me.

The next stop at *Abu Sahar Bakery* required a team effort to stretch an oven-hot roti bread between us whilst someone else slathered ghee (clarified butter) all over it and another sprinkled jaggery (unrefined sugar) onto the butter. Then it was swiftly folded, Swiss roll style, so we could all tear off pieces to try. A sugar sandwich! It was, I admit, delicious but just the bread on its own would have been fantastic.

The sugar-high continued with a visit to *Sri Krishna Sweets* for *mysore pak,* a gram flour-sugar-ghee golden brown biscuit, not unlike Scottish tablet. The display of colourful sweets was too tempting for most of us but *chivdaa/chudwaa,* a savoury snack combining fried lentils, cereals and sev was also passed round.

We stopped for a swift palate cleanser of fresh sugar cane juice with lemon and ginger before heading off to *Sind Punjab*. The familiar grilled chicken tikka is an institution here. Cooked to order, it was tasty and juicy and came with all the traditional accompaniments, including a *masala papad,* a crisp lentil disc topped with fresh coriander, tomatoes and onions; *chaat masala,* a mint yoghurt sauce; *chana masala,* chickpea gravy; a buttered *naan* bread, and *lachha paratha*, a whole wheat bread. After so much sugar, we fell upon this savoury feast and everyone said yes to second helpings.

For our final dessert we watched the chef at *Chatori Gali* create our *jalebis*. These fried ribbons of twirled batter are made with refined flour, yeast and saffron, and coated in sugar syrup. Hard to resist, especially with the accompaniments – *rabri* a dense, sweet milky confection with dried fruits, and *matka kulfi*, a pistachio flavoured Indian ice cream.

No wonder our guide handed out certificates of congratulation on completing this eating marathon. Hugely enjoyable and great fun, but more vegetables next time please!

30

Diving into the River

Losing yourself in the crowd. That wonderful feeling of being part of a community at a live concert. The music is loud, everyone around you knows the words and you're giving it back to the singer with all the madness in your soul. Brue Springsteen fans know what I'm talking about. The pandemic swiftly robbed music fans of this pleasure and left the musicians bereft too.

It would be easy to assume that it was all so different back in 2016. Dialling down the anxiety over ticket availability is never possible, but after a pandemic, when attendance at any show will feel like a reunion of lost souls? The ticket stakes will never be higher. Being a Bruce Springsteen fan is a tough call. If you have a friend that is a Bruce Springsteen fan, then please be kind. Take it from me, whenever a tour announcement is imminent they go on a roller-coaster ride of emotions. If they happen to live in a place that is never likely to figure in the tour schedule then even more understanding is required.

Let my own behaviour be my witness, ahead of *The River Tour 2016*. My friends in Dubai, and certainly my long-suffering husband became used to conducting a conversation with the top of my head because I was constantly checking my mobile phone under the table for leaked news of rumoured tour dates to Europe.

Start a social media campaign to bring the Boss to Dubai, suggested Tim. Nah. I had no time to waste on such a hopeless endeavour. There are more worthy places that have yet to see Bruce Springsteen perform live. Europe, however is known to be a favourite with the main man. Cities in Scandinavia, Italy and Ireland have famously hosted the if-you-weren't-at-that-one-you missed-THE-one-to-top-all-the-others kind of concert. The truth is every concert is a stand out, historical event for the devotee and this tour would be no exception.

The River Tour celebrated the thirty-fifth anniversary of Springsteen's iconic 1980 double album release and was in support of *The Ties That Bind: The River Collection box set*, a must-have for any fan's collection.

The tour had kicked off across North America at the start of the year and European fans had been drooling over photos and links on social media for weeks. The superlatives had been flowing like the legendary River itself from Pittsburgh to Atlanta, via Chicago, Washington, Boston, Florida and all the rest. By all accounts, the front man had shrugged off his then sixty-six years by reinvigorating a double album of fan-favourite music with the consummate skill of a seasoned entertainer and all round great guy.

How much longer could he continue to do this? We already knew that the next release was a solo project, although who could have guessed it would be another three years before the sublime *Western Stars* album would be released? There is something altogether wonderful about Bruce with the full E Street Band behind him and the *River Tour 2016* could be the last chance to experience that for a while, so naturally no die-hard fan wanted to miss it.

As witnesses took to Twitter to report the greatest, the longest, the most transformative, the tightest, loosest, roof-raising, booty-shaking, nuanced performance EVER, the cry from Europe rang out loud and clear. Yes, but when is he bringing the show to a city near me?

When solid information is missing, the vacuum will always be filled and Springsteen fans with hungry hearts are a captive audience. The rumours often turn out to be sort of right in the end, but when there are so many conflicting whispers it becomes difficult to know which ones originate from a plausible source and which are just in it for their own ego. A messenger passing information on in good faith can soon be blamed if the reports turn out to be fantasy.

It usually goes something like this.

'What did you hear?'

'Well, my cousin was in a bar with a friend that used to work down the road from the Italian promoter, and she happened to be looking over his shoulder as he was ticking off a list of dates and venues on the back of an envelope. Not official yet, but this source is rock solid... blah, blah, blah.'

There was a small window of opportunity in these situations because rumours could become official in the wink of young girl's eye, and the impact on hotel prices in the tour cities was immediate. Consequently, those that had some experience in these matters were, even at this early stage, researching flights to likely cities and googling budget hotels in the vicinity of a relevant stadium. Securing a room either side of a speculative date, on a no-payment-up-front-and-no-penalty-on-cancellation basis, was a godsend.

Being in Dubai just ramped up the anxiety level. When should we fly out to catch the UK dates? Where should we fly to? Annoyingly, reliable information on the European stops was only announced country by country. It was rumoured that the UK announcements were next. By lucky chance, early on a Friday morning my Twitter feed caught the first news of the confirmed May and June UK schedule. Two minutes later my partner in Bruce crime in Yorkshire confirmed the tentative hotel booking in Manchester, made on a lucky guess, weeks back. Meanwhile, we grabbed the only two reasonably priced rooms left in Coventry. So far, so good, but tickets for concerts in these cities still had to be secured.

At the time I didn't know if I'd be waving from the riverside, or drowning in tears should the Ticketmaster river run dry before May. That was a whole other story, but in the meantime, onwards to India.

31

Visit to Kerala

From the air our first glimpse of India looked so lush and green, abundant with vegetation and water-rich. We were about to land in Cochin for a five-night trip to Kerala. Only three and half hours by plane, but such a different landscape from the desert city of Dubai.

It was late when we checked in to our hotel but dinner was still possible. The menu at the curiously named, *Museum Restaurant* appeared promising but the place was empty and slightly creepy. The concept which hopefully didn't extend to the food seemed to invite diners to eat amongst display cases containing various ancient artefacts, tools, and decorative objects. It was all very dark and uninviting so we headed for the brighter lights of the more casual option. The lone waiter on duty didn't seem to take offence at our departure.

A freshly cooked chicken tikka for me and lamb curry for Tim. Rather good but not typical Keralan fare. We were saving that for tomorrow's lunch. We had already researched the venue and the advice was to get there early. We might need to curtail the morning sightseeing tour but how to break the bad news to our super keen tour guide and driver?

We decided to make them aware of the importance of lunch as soon as we met. Tim set the situation out very clearly at 10am. We would like a whistle-stop trip of the highlights but we needed to be at *Shappu Curry* by 12.30pm. We supplied the address as they didn't seem to know the place. It had been brought to our attention by the chef, Rick Stein during his television series on Indian food. We'd left nothing to chance and even found the relevant extract of the show on YouTube the night before, making a note of every detail.

It was hard to get any sense of where our hotel was in relation to the city centre, and even after a couple of days we were none the wiser. Cochin is set out over a series of islands linked by bridges. The rule of thumb is that everywhere you want to get to is generally at least half an hour's drive from wherever you are. Roadworks for the construction of a metro system added to journey times but with the first phase of the project due to be operational in three months, the end was definitely in sight.

Our tour started at Fort Cochin and the church of St Francis, the oldest European church in the country, built in 1503. The Portuguese explorer Vasco da Gama had been buried in the church but his remains were later removed and laid to rest in Lisbon. Our knowledgeable guide was explaining this, and giving us much more historical detail as we stood outside but I was more interested in people-watching.

In the bright light and heat of the day the vibrantly coloured saris worn by local women appeared so attractive after the sober national dress of the Middle East. Every woman was dressed for a party, yet this was everyday attire. Femininity and the female form, celebrated in jewel-bright colours and shimmering, floating fabrics was a beautiful, joyful sight.

The famous Chinese fishing nets, now a major tourist attraction, but introduced to the area by explorers in the 14th century, were a short walk away from the church. For a small fee of a hundred rupees (£1) we went on board one of the boats and helped pull on the weighted ropes to lift the huge, horizontal fishing nets out of the water. Fresh fish and a host of souvenirs are sold by the waterside and it felt like an ambush as the eager salesmen did their level best to convince us to buy their stuff.

On to the Dutch Palace, built in 1555. This houses exquisite murals depicting Hindu temple stories. No photography was allowed so our guide had to be diligent in explaining the detail. The heat made it impossible to concentrate on what he was saying so this was a quick walk-through in the end. Besides, it was almost time for lunch.

We have to thank Rick Stein and his televised odysseys for several memorably authentic holiday meals and *Shappu Curry* was another outstanding example. *Karimeen* is a local fish and one way of serving this Keralan speciality is to first cover it with a rich, red spice paste and then wrap and steam the fish in a banana leaf. We ate this dish at a couple of other places during our trip but the *Shappu Curry* version was the best.

The parcel of fish was unwrapped at the table and the flesh gently eased from the bones with a bare hand. Another banana leaf served as a plate, so that rice and a series of condiments could be added in small piles. We were the only tourists in the place that day. We treated the guide and driver to lunch too and they seemed more than happy with the choice. Eating with my hands was not for me but Tim took to it immediately. The secret of success is to roll small amounts of rice and condiment into a ball, using your thumb to pitch it into your mouth. Watching this unfold made me feel very uneasy. Sometime back, I suspect a well-meaning nursery school teacher probably covered my hands with paint and tried to encourage me to be messily creative. Knowing little me I would probably have burst into tears at such an indignity. Without the backup cutlery I had in my bag, this meal might have ended in similar scenes.

On the way to the Dutch Palace we had driven through Mattancherry, the Jewish area of Cochin, which has its own synagogue and a main street full of interesting looking shops. We decided to go back and explore this area in the evening when we had more time. Cochin gives equal respect to all faiths. I expected to see evidence of the Hindu, Christian, Roman Catholic and Muslim religions but Cochin seemed just as proud of its Jewish heritage too. I hadn't expected that.

Kerala's herb and spice trade dates back hundreds of years and even today the international market for these ingredients is a key driver of the regional economy. Locally grown pepper, cardamom, turmeric, nutmeg, cloves, cinnamon, ginger, tamarind and curry leaves are highly prized, both for their flavour and beneficial medicinal qualities.

Everywhere we went we had to reassure anxious waiters that contrary to popular belief, many Europeans like spicy food, so please bring it on! Tasty, with spice, rather than hot with chilli was our experience of the Keralan vegetable and seafood dishes we tried.

Coconut is an essential and plentiful ingredient. The milk adds a soothing richness and depth to savoury dishes, whilst shavings of coconut might be mixed through a plate of finely cut fried vegetables or grated into a side dish for added texture. Sour notes of tamarind, lime, vinegar or unripe mango also pop up from time to time to keep your palate guessing.

Over the past months we had amassed an untidy collection of spices for our Dubai kitchen cupboard. The identifying labels had long gone and in the haste that often accompanied my kitchen prep, the contents had spilled into the large tray that served as a holding pen. At the Women's Co-operative Spice Market I found a practical solution in the *masala dabba*. A stainless steel round box containing six smaller pots is an essential feature of the Indian kitchen as it allows the cook to store and locate individual spices with ease. A little bit of best price banter ensued before a deal was struck and the parcel wrapped.

Our charming and cheeky shop assistant was on a mission though, because we were treading in the footsteps of greatness. As the newspaper cuttings around the shop announced, HRH Prince Charles and his blessed Camilla had graced this place with their presence, and we were therefore invited to consider purchasing some of the pashminas and handmade jewellery that so pleased the Duchess of Cornwall.

I was ushered to an upstairs room to peruse the wares whilst Tim examined a guitar he found on display. This was a helpful distraction as the chief saleswoman and her sidekick were so enthralled by Tim and his impromptu strumming they both left me in peace.

The next morning it was farewell to Cochin and onward to Alleppy jetty, a two–hour drive away, to board a houseboat for an overnight cruise though the famous lakes and lagoons known as the Keralan backwaters.

The journey through the countryside and villages was fascinating. We passed areas where workers were laying out coir mats to dry in the sun, showing that every part of the coconut is useful. Cashew nut trees at the side of the road were a revelation, as our guide showed us that the nuts are harvested from the seed pod of a juicy yellow fruit.

We had to slow down when a procession of elephants, led from a Hindu temple and crowds of revellers in their wake, signalled a festival event was in full swing. The women wore special white saris and it all seemed a very jolly, musical, family occasion. Our driver was able to pull over so we could get out and take it all in which was both exciting and unexpected.

An overnight cruise on a houseboat had the potential to be wonderfully romantic and relaxing, and if it had been a day trip ours would have been a wonderful experience. The boats, and there are many of them, cruise along at a leisurely pace revealing everyday life along the riverside. There is much to see but when the heat of the day overwhelms, leaning back in a comfy chair on a covered sun deck, a cold drink to hand is pretty blissful. Sadly, the bedroom and bathroom overnight accommodation on our boat lacked the basic comforts that most tourists would expect, but at least the food didn't disappoint.

One of the three-man houseboat crew produced simple, local dishes from a tiny kitchen. Our lunch was a feast with vegetable dishes of dal, okra and a delightful beetroot *sambar* easily outshining the *karimeen* fish which was sadly overcooked. The star of the show was a *thoran*, a delicious mix of fried, finely shredded cabbage, snake beans, carrot, onion, and green chillies, flavoured with black mustard seeds, curry leaves and shards of coconut. I could have eaten a whole bowl of it.

At one point the boat was moored at a village so we could have a wander along the bank. The villagers do their fresh food shopping in the early morning at the riverside, where fish and fruit sellers bob close to the bank in small canoes. We also came upon a ramshackle bar where we could investigate the notorious toddy, the alcoholic home brew made from coconut sap. The proprietor gave Tim a complimentary glass to try. We both had a taste to be polite but it was pretty rough.

Onwards by car to our next and final stop, the lakeside village of Kumarakom and a beautiful spa resort. A tranquil haven of landscaped gardens, stunning views and comfortable deluxe accommodation was greatly appreciated after the somewhat charmless houseboat facilities.

A spot of poolside relaxation and a cooling dip eased us back into holiday mode. The resort employs an army of gardeners to keep the grounds immaculate at all times. I loved the ingenious umbrella-like contraptions they wore on their heads as sun protection. One of those would be really handy in Dubai.

Tim's pre-birthday celebrations started with a cake delivered to our room soon after our arrival. How did they know? On closer inspection, the icing indicated this was a welcome cake for both of us. How very thoughtful. We tucked in, thinking the rest could be enjoyed for dessert later on. If we had known this was to be the first of three cakes to appear over the next twenty-four hours we might not have been quite so enthusiastic. Meanwhile, there was dinner to consider and we were in the mood to explore.

A Keralan contact had given me a list of suggested restaurants to try in this area. One called *Thali* was in the nearby town of Kottayam, just a taxi ride away. Their dinner speciality is stuffed *dosas* and we were the only tourists trying them in this popular, but basic family restaurant.

A *dosa* is similar to a savoury pancake, but made with rice batter and black lentils. Tim's had a chicken filling and I tried the vegetable one. Both were deliciously fresh and bursting with spice and flavour. Two contrasting accompaniments were provided – one of coconut and coriander and the other more of a gravy. With two cups of black tea it was proper comfort food. Dinner for two that night came to less than £2.50. What a bargain!

The next day we'd arranged to go on a sunset cruise around the lake but before we left to go, a second cake was delivered to the room, for this was indeed Tim's birthday. Good timing, as we could share this amongst the other guests gathered at the jetty for afternoon tea. I had pre-arranged a swanky birthday dinner at the *Vivanta by Taj* hotel up the road so we decided to forgo the cake at this stage. A wise decision.

The setting for Tim's birthday meal was certainly impressive. We had the best table in the outdoor restaurant, overlooking the lagoon and right in front of a performance area. Traditional live music and dance was taking place that evening. Perfect! My one fear when making the booking was that we would be a feast for peckish mosquitoes but the restaurant staff were diligent in keeping the pests at bay. Every fifteen minutes or so an attendant would walk back and forth swinging a metal container of burning citronella, creating wafts of protective vapour. This strategy worked a treat.

Dinner was outstanding. Tim went for *Pollichathu*, the Keralan fish, steamed in a banana leaf but I was keen to try one of the gorgeous sounding lamb dishes. I chose *Ghosht Hazaari*, Hyderabadi style mutton with ginger and mint. It was meltingly tender and exceptionally generous with ginger. On advice from the waiter I changed my first choice of coconut rice to a pulao with peas that would better compliment the lamb. Dinner was one of those special experiences where the mood, place and quality of food were in perfect harmony.

When we arrived, the waiter's knowing smile at our name told me that dessert was already taken care of. I decided not to break the news, ahead of the arrival of what I suspected would be the third birthday cake. Fortunately, the band were coming to the end of their performance so we asked for extra plates and forks and dished out generous slices for the musicians.

We were nearly at the end of our adventure but we had some time the next morning to drive to the spectacular waterfalls of Anthirapally. There was an unforgiving and steep walk to the gorge, and the climb back up in the heat of the day is not for the faint-hearted but it was definitely worth it. It was impressive to see the number of local female visitors scrambling over the rocks and balancing along the steeper slopes in highly decorative saris and totally unsuitable sandals.

We took the chance to catch our breath at rest points on the return. Local teenagers on a school visit spotted the chance to practise their English and were very keen to take selfies with us. It was all a bit surprising but totally charming. That just about sums up our trip to Kerala.

32

Three Days in Budapest

With elegant cafés, stunning architecture and history around every corner, there are a million reasons to visit Budapest. Our visit to Hungary's esteemed capital city was a chance to catch up with old friends from the UK in a fabulous destination. By good chance, flight times to and from Dubai and the UK gave us all a three-day window to sample a flavour of what makes Budapest special. Not enough time to see it all but we certainly gave it our best shot.

Budapest sits on the River Danube and is a city of two halves, Buda and Pest. Both sides offer spectacular views and attractions but are quite distinct in character. The Pest side is where the majority of the city's hotels, restaurants, shops, and bars are located, and is a great base from which to explore. The Hungarian Parliament Building and the Opera House, both architectural gems are also there. The higher Buda side has even more spectacular historic buildings and fantastic views. The funicular railway is a charming way to get up to Castle Hill and the various vantage points.

While we were waiting for our friends to arrive we did a quick recce around our area in Pest and found we were within walking distance of St Stephen's Basilica and a view of the impressive Royal Palace across the river, which is floodlit after dark.

It took me precisely five minutes to discover that *Gerbeaud*, the famous café and cake shop was close to our hotel, though perhaps its very proximity made us complacent about opening times. Cake cravings need to be satisfied before 9pm to avoid acute disappointment at this upmarket establishment, as we discovered on night two. On day three we weren't taking any chances. We ordered cakes and sundaes shortly after breakfast. I loved the Esterhazy cake, a light-as-air layered sponge, with buttercream, walnuts and a feather-iced topping. This is by no means the only quality cake show in town, though.

With beautiful blue skies and temperatures inching up to a promising 23°C on our first morning, we headed off on foot to the atmospheric Jewish Quarter, passing the Great Synagogue, with its beautiful Moorish style decoration and distinctive towers. The largest synagogue in the world and its associated museum was closed, due to the Jewish Passover holiday but with such glorious weather none of us fancied stepping out of the sunshine anyway, except for breakfast of course.

The main covered food market was just across the road and is a glorious celebration of the nation's produce, with stall after stall of colourful fruit and vegetables, hundreds of deli sausages, pickles and the staple spice of paprika. Hungary is a nation of makers so home-produced leather bags, wooden toys, hand crafted jewellery and embroidered goods on the upper floor were interesting to browse through too. It made a refreshing change from the usual imports and chain stores that dominate Dubai, and the prices were realistic too.

When the weather changed on our final morning, a handy flea market offered shelter from the pouring rain and harsh wind.

Here the prices were less good and no one seemed willing to negotiate downwards for a sale, which was surprising as the quality and provenance of some of the goods was dubious, to say the least.

The maze of streets in and around the Jewish Quarter are home to the Ruin bars and clubs in Budapest, so-called because they operate in the shabby chic of abandoned buildings. Parties on a nightly basis take place behind the battered doors and decrepit facades. The ghosts of the previous inhabitants are very present here and especially in and around a courtyard, where part of the original ghetto wall was reconstructed as a stark memorial to victims of the Holocaust. A more beautiful metal tree sculpture stands in the garden behind the Great Synagogue. The family names of murdered victims are etched on its leaves.

An even more affecting reminder of the associated atrocities that took place in Budapest during 1944-45 can be seen by the riverside. It was here that Jewish men, women, and children were lined up at the very edge and shot so their bodies fell into the water. This dark history is illustrated through metal representations of the victim's shoes, randomly placed along the edge of the promenade. Many had flowers, stones and candles recently placed in them. The power of commonplace, individual personal objects bearing witness to such terrible events was extremely moving.

Behind our hotel we joined the crowds choosing their dinner at a lively craft and traditional food market. Hearty Hungarian specialities included goulash soup served in a round loaf, confit goose leg with red cabbage, paprika-spiced sausage and pork knuckle with roasted peppers. Free live entertainment was provided by a Simon and Garfunkel tribute act. Presumably, Paul Simon, being the son of Hungarian immigrants offered a flimsy bridge over cultural waters.

Cheap and cheerful food stalls one night, and a fabulous dinner the next at the smart *Kollázs Brasserie* at the Four Seasons hotel. Dishes of melt in the mouth scallops, foie gras terrine, belly pork, lamb shank, rib-eye steak and beef cheek with a goulash jus were faultless. Amazingly, we still had room for desserts of chocolate lava cake, crème brulée and a dulce de leche tart. Prices per head, with wine and coffee were a reasonable £35.

Music and musical heritage is everywhere in Budapest – from the Ferenc Liszt Memorial Museum to instrumentalists on street corners. The best of these was the gentleman playing *The Flight of the Bumble Bee* on a series of glasses filled with water. We also enjoyed a violinist playing for his own pleasure at the Fisherman's Bastion and three police brass bands, in a competitive play-off near the Royal Palace.

Taking the waters in Budapest is a must, and after all the walking we did, a therapeutic way to spend a morning. We headed off to the *Gellért Baths,* a grand Art Nouveau temple to thermal spa pleasure. We found several pools of varying heat, sauna rooms, an ice-cold plunge bath, plus a swimming facility and special massage room. We were quite conservative on what we tried but it was a treat to take in the surrounding grandeur and afterwards we all floated out, suitably de-stressed from the mineral-rich soaking.

Three days was just enough to get a flavour of Budapest but with more time we might have explored a museum or art gallery, maybe taken a tour of the Parliament Building or spent a day at Margaret Island. And definitely eaten more cake.

33

Tales from the Riverbank

Back in Dubai, after a two-week, high octane visit to the UK and France, it was no wonder I was feeling discombobulated.

In just a fortnight, through two countries, we had crossed many rivers to visit two graves, attend two Bruce Springsteen concerts, stand for a show at London's Globe Theatre, celebrate with our nearest and dearest, reconnect with dear friends, make new ones, meet the youngest members of the family, and explore the charming French city of Rennes. The last, all the while blissfully unaware that we would need to hire a car, as due to labour strikes, there would be no trains to take us to Paris and a flight back to Dubai the next day. Irony alert. Ah, Europe, how I've missed you and your freedom to withdraw your labour!

In a packed schedule which I always knew would trigger some big emotions, settling back to expat life in such a different landscape took some re-adjustment.

Our host country had entered the holy month of Ramadan, but my thoughts were fixed on Europe, specifically the debate and outcome of the EU referendum and the flow of Bruce Springsteen's concert tour, the latter accessed via social media through the sharing of pictures and set lists by the faithful, to the faithful. So, until both these momentous events concluded I remained in an unusual state of mental flux, neither here nor there.

Catching Springsteen's tour had been a project, months in the making and uniting a group of us over several continents and time zones. We were holidaying in Kerala when tickets for the UK shows went on sale. Our hotel room resembled the Houston control centre with all devices booted up and ready for ticket drop at UK time. We also had a Skype link back to our friends in Yorkshire, who were also trying to purchase as insurance against flaky connections to the Ticketmaster site. It was a triumph. Standing tickets for two shows. We were all going to be dancing in the dark with the Boss. Metaphorically and quite possibly, literally.

When I book tickets for an outdoor concert in the UK, the assumption is always that the sun will shine. It rarely does when the date finally comes around and the destination is Manchester. Bruce said as much from the stage of the Etihad stadium and insisted he and the band wouldn't have it any other way. Well, sorry Bruce, but I beg to differ there. Pouring rain plays havoc with the hair and the planned outfit, and we girls do like to look our best for you. Manchester is a cruel mistress. Just two days before the show, we enjoyed a canal-side walk and drinks in glorious sunshine.

A week later in Coventry, the skies stayed dull over the Ricoh arena but the evening was dry and almost warm, or was that the heat from the thousands of fans around us? What is the chance that two concert-goers, standing directly behind us in the pit would turn out to be a couple we met five years before in Langkawi? The power of Bruce is great indeed.

127

My personal river tour highlights were those collected close to the Thames, the Mersey, the Avon, the Ure, and the Vilaine in France. A kaleidoscope of mixed emotions, prompted by the following:

Seeing old friends and close family at my mum's memorial service and laughing in the sunshine with them afterwards.

Walking along Bankside from Tate Modern to Shakespeare's magnificent Globe Theatre.

Eating dinner with both our boys at the always excellent *Joe Allen's* in Covent Garden.

Strolling through the 18th century landscaped *Parc du Thabor* in Rennes.

Being at the rail in Manchester when Bruce played *Santa Claus is Comin' to Town* – in May. Shout out to the fan who tried the long shot of dressing as Santa for the night. It worked.

Chatting to the lovely girl and her mum behind us in the pit line in Manchester. Mum had her phone on the selfie setting so her daughter could put on her make-up (good trick). Later, her daughter was pulled up on stage for a dance with the Boss and handled her moment with exceptional grace.

Tim loving the whole experience of standing for three hours to watch a Shakespeare play, and why didn't I say it would be a show? I seriously undersold Emma Rice's production of *A Midsummer Night's Dream*.

Appreciating every morsel of food we consumed in Rennes. In France, even cheese on toast is elevated to three types, melted onto the best bread in the world.

Visiting the city of Bath – independent shopping at its best but even the chain stores seemed above average in range and layout, and all walkable in the centre.

Enjoying how John, Paul, George and Ringo are celebrated in Liverpool. Only in this city could you find a hotel called *A Hard Day's Night* and quite right too.

Hearing *Point Blank* and *Drive All Night* sung live at different shows for the first time. Two Springsteen songs I've loved for years.

Loving pretty much everything about the *Balthazar Hotel* in Rennes which proved to be a boutique hotel with heart. Tim watched as a homeless guy entered the lobby to help himself to the edibles on display. Staff let him continue for a bit and then gave him a glass of water before leading him out.

Eating Sunday lunch with friends in a sunny pub garden. After a year in Dubai, largely spent avoiding the heat, we both got sunburnt in a single afternoon in North Yorkshire.

34

All Shook Up

Four and half years after the referendum result, a fragile trade deal between the United Kingdom and the European Union finally limped over the finish line on Christmas Eve 2020. Bitter wrangling on both sides over the terms of the withdrawal agreement, and then protracted negotiations surrounding a trade deal had gone on for so long, world events, not least a health emergency had stolen the limelight and upstaged Brexit's leading players. It was all so different, hearing the result from Dubai on the morning of 24th June 2016.

I woke early and switched on the television to see shocked news presenters delivering the results. Fifty two percent of the UK had voted to leave the EU and therefore we were out. Following weeks of bitter and fractious campaigning, and a slew of misinformation, Vote Leave had narrowly triumphed over Remain. The Remoaners, as they would soon be labelled, would just have to live with it.

At the time I couldn't decide which was worse – hearing about the fallout and mood of my home country from afar or being in the thick of it. The consequences of a Leave victory seemed to have come as a complete surprise to the winning side, never mind the rest of us. Emotionally and geographically the UK was fractured.

David Cameron, the PM, ardent Remainer and the architect of the referendum had resigned, the leader of the opposition was about to be ousted and Scotland, who voted to remain in the EU was considering its options. Nothing about this had been predicted by the commentators, the pollsters or the pundits.

I don't recall a single moment in the debates where anyone was quizzed on what might happen if Scottish voters went in a different direction. Or if Cameron ended up on the losing side? What exactly was the plan and who was in charge?

It was heartbreaking to hear about the divisions in communities and even within families and friends over leaving the EU. Charismatic and decisive leadership might pull the country together but it was nowhere to be found.

Hours after the results were known, a petition calling for a second referendum was circulating on social media. Innocents were signing it without wondering for a second who the originator was. Turned out it was a student having a laugh, who suddenly found thousands of others were taking him seriously. Boris Johnson was about to take this stunt as a mission statement.

Much as I disagreed with the arguments for leaving the EU, I did not see how holding a second referendum would solve anything. The issue was too important to be reduced to such a simplistic leave or remain choice when the consequences were so devastating.

It was shortly after this that we headed for Bulgaria, an EU member since 1995.

35

A Break in Bulgaria

The Eid holiday that followed Ramadan offered an opportunity for a short trip away, but where to go?

We'd thought about northern India but arriving at the start of the rainy season wasn't a great idea. A Korean colleague of Tim's encouraged us to consider Seoul but the potential for heavy rain there too put us off. A five-hour flight to Sofia, Bulgaria's capital, looked much more appealing.

Our holiday apartment was one of the best and most comfortable we've ever had, and also the least expensive. We couldn't help thinking that Bulgaria might be missing a trick by not marketing Sofia more aggressively as a value for money destination.

The main sights and monuments revealed thousands of years of history, multiple religious beliefs and political regimes. Ruins, and in some cases, rebuilt Roman ruins, lay in the shadow of the more extravagant edifices associated with the Communist era and stark Brutalist architecture of the 1970s. Bulgaria only became a Republic in 1990.

We noted, with grim humour, the EU flag proudly flying over the official sites. Perhaps the EU funding no longer available to the UK could be put to good use in improving the state of Sofia's pavements. Lethally uneven, the broken slabs, holes and alarming dips in the path ways would make a British council chief quake at the potential for litigation. I have never spent so much time in a new place with my eyes fixed on the ground in order to avoid tripping over. At night, with street lighting at a minimum, the dangers to life and limb were multiplied. No wonder we didn't see any disabled residents or small children on the streets.

Natural and man-made beauty overlook this city. The Vitosha mountains were clearly visible in the distance but I found the golden statue of the generously bosomed patron saint on her column a much more arresting sight. Installed in 2000, the sensuous Saint Sofia, arms outstretched towards the traffic in benediction, replaced a likeness of Lenin that had previously kept a watchful eye over the city.

The Bulgarian language could be a barrier for English speaking visitors. The written word is in Cyrillic script and the average taxi driver, public servant or small shopkeeper does not speak or understand more than the most basic of English. That said, we got by without too many problems.

We joined a free walking tour of the main sites led by a student keen to engage with visitors. Our guide spoke near perfect English, and could explain the city's history and traditions in a nuanced and illuminating way. His overview of the Square of Tolerance stuck in my mind. We were standing outside the former state owned TZUM department store, a Communist era retail temple of sorts. From that spot we could also see a cathedral, a mosque, an orthodox church and a synagogue. During the Second World War Bulgaria stood alone as the only Eastern European country to protect and save its entire Jewish population of 48,000 souls from certain death. Government officials refused to co-operate with the Nazi order for deportation, and religious leaders from other denominations, and even ordinary citizens protested against the race hate and murder. Our guide's explanation of the triumph that stemmed from this rare act of collective humanity was so powerful I couldn't help but burst into spontaneous applause.

There are two main food markets in Sofia but only one worthy of attention. The exterior of the covered food market looked impressive but inside it felt soulless with surprisingly few customers. A little further up the road the so-called Women's Market, where fruit and vegetable sellers called out their prices and small traders dealt in ceramics and snacks, was much more lively and atmospheric.

Despite the charitable traditions of the various religions, the city's poorest citizens and stray animals go unnoticed and those that are barely surviving have to be alive to any opportunity. Aside from the taxi scams that awaited the unwitting tourist, we saw static beggars and also several dogs, the latter roaming independently, looking for crumbs of comfort. We picked up a map of Sofia, cunningly illustrated in cartoon style, naming the area around the train station as Robbery Central and using a symbol of a moving handbag to underline the point with disarming honesty. No different to most European cities, I guess.

The food was a surprise. Not the carb-heavy menus I was expecting, as Bulgarians don't always fill up on bread and potatoes. Salads are a popular starter and most menus had a list of choices. My favourite was *Shopska*, a delicious traditional salad of fresh tomatoes, cucumbers, roasted red peppers, spring onions and parsley, in a light dressing. A crumbly white cheese, called *Sirene,* similar to Greek feta cheese, was sprinkled over the vegetables. Meat is usually grilled and dressed with a savoury sauce. All very wholesome, fresh and delicious. Judging from the crowds of locals at the two restaurants we tried, many also shared our opinion.

Shtastliveca was a recommended restaurant and we liked it so much we went back twice. Another, charmingly named *Made in Home,* was a little more rustic but the desserts were outstanding. We shared a piece of their creamy raspberry cheesecake with a chocolate and blueberry crumb base. My mouth waters at the memory. Local wines, especially the reds, were superb and prices at most places incredibly low.

On the train journey to Bulgaria's second city, Plovdiv we tried *banitsa,* a savoury breakfast snack comprising a tough filo pastry case, stuffed with white cheese. The homemade version might be more digestible, but we couldn't get down more than a bite each of the one we purchased from the Bulgarian equivalent of Greggs. *Ayran,* a salted yoghurt drink had more potential, though the full fat version was too rich for my taste and undrinkable after five minutes outside a fridge.

Plovdiv, European Capital of Culture 2019 is smaller than Sofia but the town has a cosmopolitan, prosperous feel to it and there was lots to see and admire on a walk round.

Different civilisations have lived in Plovdiv for more than eight thousand years and important historical evidence exists in, amongst, and below the centre of the city. It was a steep climb up to the Old Town and the main street of highly decorative buildings. Some house museum collections and others operate as workshops for artists and craftspeople. The crowning glory is the

Roman amphitheatre. On the day we visited a rock band were in rehearsal for a concert so we could only peep through the gaps at this restored treasure, uncovered in 1972 after a landslide. We concluded that allowing such a precious site to be in use as a venue for entertainment was brilliant.

We could only stay in Plovdiv for a day and the return journey to Sofia by super slow train was torture, but the magical views from the Old Town and its buildings made us want to see more of Bulgaria, a fascinating and overlooked tourist destination.

36

What's Cookin' in Kiev?

My dinner had arrived and was making me nervous. It was Chicken Kiev. We were eating at one of Kiev's best known traditional restaurants and in a burst of nostalgia I had ordered a dish I last ate in London in the late 1970s. To be honest, it gave me a bit of a thrill to know that Chicken Kiev was actually a real menu item in the city of the same name. This dish, created in Russia is well-loved in Ukraine, and exported all over the world. The whole story is a little more complicated than that as the French, various world leaders, American immigrants, tourism, and persuasive marketing all played a part in the story too.

For those who have never tried it, the dish comprises a chicken breast, flattened to accommodate a garlic butter and parsley stuffing. It is then rolled and sealed with an egg and breadcrumb coating before deep-frying to crispy, golden perfection.

Someone should have warned me in London that my dinner had the potential to injure. Back then, my innocent knife went in at just the right point to release a volcano of foaming fat from within. I just had time to notice the garlicky aroma before half a pint of boiling butter sprayed onto my chest, completing its journey down my front in meandering rivulets. Nice. No wonder Chicken Kiev made me nervous.

This time I approached my dinner with extreme caution but there was no need to worry. The butter stuffing was barely in evidence and I ended up dissecting my portion in a bid to find it.

Also on the menu that evening were plates of unusual appetisers, including miniature dumplings with a rabbit or mushroom stuffing, pickled vegetables, cured meats and neat squares of dark bread with a pork fat and olive topping. The drinks included vodka, flavoured with fiery horseradish and another with honey. I preferred the non-alcoholic drink called *uzvar* made from smoked pears. The city's hippest mixologists were using a version of this in cocktails.

Smoked prunes, offered for breakfast in our hotel had a definite hint of old ashtray which put me right off. Smoked prunes? Quirky, right? Kiev *is* quirky and it didn't take me long to get in the groove.

History, revolution, war and Ukrainian heritage are all well represented in the city's official museum collections, but the wackier offerings were much more appealing to me. The Drugstore Museum, Kiev Wax Museum and the Museum of Circus Art all beckoned but it was no contest once I heard there was a Toilet History Museum, located in a 19th century fortress.

The fortress in question sits within a depressing housing estate. I lost my way twice but those I asked seemed to know what I was looking for. Those that understood English spoke it very well. I say this but on another day someone thought I wanted to purchase a headstone when I was in fact asking the way to a war memorial, but I digress. The Toilet History Museum houses the world's largest collection of items associated with urination and defecation. Chamber pots, bowls, pans and other receptacles down the ages, through to the more sophisticated and recent urinals, flushing toilets and art pieces. There are also cabinets crammed full of decorative miniatures.

Pages of information, translated into English were pressed into my hands at the entrance, as the chief curator was busy explaining everything in fine detail to a party of visiting Russians. She was just getting to the Romans as I was leaving the premises. The translation fondly honours Thomas Crapper, the father of British plumbing furniture who is treated to his own display area. It amused me that visitors have to walk past a state of the art bathroom shop to exit the museum, a gentle reminder that most people's facilities could do with an update.

The next stop should have been more conventional, being a museum devoted to Sholom Aleichem, the Ukrainian literary giant. However, as I was the only visitor an English-speaking member of staff was immediately summoned to explain everything to me, personally. The exhibits, all housed in a single room include letters of admiration from Tolstoy, Pushkin and Chekhov as well as posters for the original Broadway production of *Fiddler on the Roof*, which is based on Sholom Aleichem's stories.

The Pinchuk Art Centre is a contemporary art gallery on several floors. When we visited they were hosting an exhibition, titled, *Loss*, a re-interpretation of themes associated with Second World War events. The most affecting of these were the sculptures depicting the Babi Yar massacre which took place during the Nazi occupation of Ukraine. The previous day I had taken the metro to the Babi Yar site, a forest ravine just outside

Kiev, where there are several moving memorials to the victims of the atrocities.

Pecherska Lavra is the most sacred site in the Orthodox Church of Ukraine. An ancient monastery comprising a complex of gold-domed churches and caves is arguably Kiev's principle historic attraction. Above ground there are fantastic views of the city whilst below, along hushed and narrow passages lie the mummified bodies of the monks that lived there from its founding in 1051.

The scale and majesty of the complex was impressive but the caves were definitely the highlight. Visitors can buy candles to light their way which adds to the creepy atmosphere. The route is very narrow and I didn't expect to see worshippers stopping to kiss the glass-topped coffins as they went. The withered hands of some of the deceased were visible through the glass. The priests at the entrance act like bouncers and are there to enforce the dress code. Women wearing trousers had to put on a wraparound skirt supplied for the purpose although, bizarrely, younger girls in short dresses caused no concern at all.

One of the prettiest streets in Kiev's old town is St Andrew's Descent, a long, winding, cobblestoned route with the church of the same name at the top, and stalls selling eclectic flea market goods, craft items, art work and souvenirs all along its length.

Time passed quickly here as we stopped to browse for something unusual and original amongst the galleries, vintage clothes shops and local makers selling their goods. We came back with a framed picture and a traditional carved wooden box.

The Besarabsky covered food market is said to be too expensive for most locals and when we visited there were hardly any takers for the bountiful displays of fruit and vegetables, smoked fish, meats and caviar.

Outside the metro stations we noticed the competition – babushkas from the rural areas, selling little pots of home-grown soft fruits and husks of sweetcorn.

It is possible to eat very well in Kiev for next to nothing and even the relatively expensive places seemed reasonable. One gem we went back to twice was *Good Wine*, a restaurant with an impressive food and drink emporium attached.

We had a delicious prosecco and grapefruit cocktail there and were so impressed with that combination we bought a bottle of the grapefruit liqueur in the shop. Grapefruit liqueur? Quirky Kiev!

37

Salalah for Eid

We were not quite through the most challenging part of the year in Dubai, when temperatures soared to plus 40°C by day, dropping only two or three degrees after sundown.

How do you cope with the summer heat? Easily the most frequently asked question, and one I asked myself before I lived in Dubai. The answer is simple. If you can't stand the heat, avoid unnecessary exposure. No one with any sense goes for casual exploratory strolls during the day or arranges meetings that might involve waiting in full sun for more than a minute or two.

By following sensible and obvious advice on sun protection and hydration the body gradually adjusts to the new conditions. I thought I would melt during my first summer in Dubai but the second was easier. Most expats leave the city during August but those who opt to stay in Dubai usually arrange frequent short trips away as a coping strategy. During 2016 one of two long weekends marking Eid in the religious calendar fell in September, so offered the perfect excuse to go somewhere cooler.

Similar to the school holiday season in the UK, flights to all destinations from Dubai suddenly go up in price for Eid, and clauses excluding the holiday from any discounted offers in Middle East hotels are writ large.

Ask anyone living in Dubai for suggestions on places to visit in Oman and they will probably list one of three destinations.

The capital city of Muscat is said to be a must-see, with its fabulous Souk and impressive historic architecture. Or they might mention Khasab in the Musandam region, a mountainous peninsula with a jagged coastline, within driving distance from Dubai. We'd enjoyed dolphin spotting on board a traditional dhow there, twice. Others had told us about Salalah, the capital city of southern Oman's Dhofar province, a two-hour flight away. They'd described the landscape there as lush. Lush? In the Middle East? How come? The trusty friends that knew their geography pointed out that as Salalah is sub-tropical it had a monsoon season that was just ending in September, when daytime temperatures were around a pleasant 27°C. It sounded perfect.

At that special time of year, even from the plane, Salalah's landscape looked strikingly abundant. As we drove to the various beauty spots the deep green colours and undulating views on show were a treat for the senses after sandy Dubai. We didn't get to see everything but the sights we experienced are unique to this region.

Walking along the beach on the first day the misty warm air felt like rain on the skin, yet it wasn't raining. The sandpipers were our entertainment and we watched them speeding along the sand looking for something to eat, before dodging the choppy waters just in time.

The next morning we hired a 4x4 and were ready to explore. By amazing coincidence, the vehicle's registration plate featured Tim's initials and year of birth. Felt like a good sign.

After the monsoon most visitors head for the hills and the scenic routes leading to caves, mountain springs and waterfalls. We had to pause in our eagerness to get to one waterhole to let a group of camels cross the road. Further on, high on a hill, a lone shepherd tending his goats was a biblical sight.

Were we in the Middle East or the North York Moors? We really didn't expect to see green and rolling hills in the same locality as coconut palms and banana plantations. The surprising contrasts continued when we turned another corner to find a scrubby desert view and a vista of low growing, bushy trees.

We had happened upon Wadi Dawkah and a park of frankincense trees, part of a site recognised by UNESCO's World Cultural and Natural Heritage List. Oman's highly prized signature perfume is made from sap, collected from the trees at various stages of their growth, mixed with coals and burnt to produce a resin. That explained the heady fragrance in the lobby of our hotel. The frankincense from Dhofar is considered to be the finest in the world and is used to perfume clothes, hair and beards. The smoke also repels mosquitoes, which is handy in this area, and it has medicinal properties too.

Salalah town itself was unremarkable so we stood for a while to watch a group of men outside a café playing a game that looked like Ludo, before admiring the immaculate exterior of the Sultan Qaboos Mosque.

We found food outside of the hotel resorts to be a bit hit and miss. We enjoyed a delicious Goan Kingfish curry at the Rotana Beach Resort but on another night in Salalah town we chose less well. We weren't the only customers tempted to try the Chinese restaurant as two girls we'd met at the airport were also hoping for the best there too. The Omani and Indian cooks in Salalah were obviously used to producing food with an international theme but they could have done with a Chinese national in this kitchen. We should have known it was game over when two pots of jasmine tea proved a challenge. It wasn't just that the restaurant only had one teapot, more to the point, the kitchen didn't know how to make jasmine tea. There were more leaves than water in this version.

On the coast road near the Marneef Cave we passed unspoilt beaches and watched as the Indian Ocean made its presence felt. Tourists could stand over a grating for a refreshing, if violent and noisy soaking, at a strategically placed blowhole. We chose a cool and quiet spot directly under an overhanging rock to watch them enjoy the shock of total saturation.

Salalah made me realise just how much I'd missed green, rolling countryside and clean, fresh air.

38

Desert Day, Spanish Night

Constant, searing summer heat kept me mostly indoors over July and August but once it started to abate, I dared to venture out of my air-conditioned hibernation. Experienced, sensible friends high-tailed it out of Dubai when the heat was on, only returning once the worst was over. Staying put for the most part had been an interesting challenge.

A couple of writing projects kept me motivated to use this significant and precious block of time while I could. Dubai is a feast or famine sort of place. Entertainment-wise, nothing for weeks and then suddenly everything ramps up. Special occasions, invitations, recommendations and new attractions all come along at once to fill the spare time.

Dubai's spanking new Opera House had opened its doors a couple of months before and I'd been looking out for a show in the first season that we would both enjoy. Then a friend recommended lunch at the luxury *Al Maha* desert resort. Time to seize the day. Unusually, both website booking systems were functioning as they should and before I knew it I'd secured a fabulous lunch package in the desert, and tickets for a world class flamenco show at the Opera House. Both, on the same date. Like I said, feast or famine.

First to the feast. *Al Maha* is one of those out of town attractions that cause most pleasure-seekers to choke on their champagne when they find out how much it costs to actually stay there. The lunch package by Dubai standards is affordable though, and perhaps because of this I was a wee bit doubtful that it would be anything special. I couldn't have been more wrong. The location, hidden deep within Dubai's Desert Conservation Reserve made a visit a proper adventure. The complex of tents that surrounded the resort's suites and spa were only visible after a considerable drive through the sand dunes. Once there, the Bedouin heritage design of the public areas did not appear strikingly sumptuous or ostentatious, which would have struck a false note. Nevertheless, the interiors were well-appointed and attractive. Just what you need to relax and indulge.

It was still too hot to eat lunch on the terrace overlooking the desert but the main restaurant was just as inviting, and the white linen tablecloths promised the fine dining experience we'd hoped for. Lunch was a three-course affair and though the menu options were fairly standard there was ample choice. So why did we come away thinking that this was amongst the best meals we'd eaten in Dubai?

First, the kitchen used top quality ingredients and prepared simple dishes, very, very well. There was nothing particularly complicated about a salmon fishcake and a bowl of pumpkin soup but I've eaten poor examples of both in other places. Here, the soup was creamy, well-seasoned and actually tasted of pumpkin, the fish cake coating, crisp and golden, with a satisfying ratio of fish to potato. Everything looked and tasted the best it could be.

At first I wondered if the Hollandaise sauce that accompanied my fish cake had split, but the unusual texture turned out to be finely grated lemongrass, creating a subtle Asian twist. I'm not sure the addition was entirely necessary but I was deeply impressed that the waiter could supply the answer to the question, which added up to the third reason this was such an enjoyable meal. Well-trained, helpful staff always take dining out to a different level.

Our main courses were equally impressive. There was nowhere to hide with our fillet steak and grilled lamb chops and both dishes looked perfect and the portions generous. I don't usually order fillet steak because it lacks the flavour of the fattier cuts but this was another triumph. The best was yet to come, so just as well we'd left a bit of room.

Desserts were a little more elaborate and the pastry chef made it difficult to choose. It was a tough call but we went for a yuzu and ginger crème brûlée and a cocoa nib dacquoise. The latter was essentially a layered meringue, served with a passion fruit curd and banana sorbet. Both were divine. We were just tucking in when a third dessert arrived. No mistake. Chef had sent us a complimentary chocolate fondant tart because he thought we just might like to try that as well. He was right. How often does that happen?

The suites at *Al Maha* have private pools and courtyards but day guests can use the outdoor pool area at the spa. Wildlife roam around freely outside and we encountered a family of gazelles grazing close by. A cheeky one even sauntered through the pool area while we were taking a breather on a sun lounger.

The desert is about an hour's drive from the centre of Dubai, making the creation of a nearby futuristic city an even more remarkable achievement. The approach to the new Opera House and the coloured lighting and water sculptures outside, another example of Dubai's supercharged development programme.

We had come to see the flamenco superstar, Sara Baras touring her latest show, *Voces*. Lots of the female ticket-holders appeared to be channelling their inner Spanish diva in their wow-factor outfits. You can never be overdressed in Dubai! I'm glad we arrived early to both soak up the pre-show atmosphere and appreciate the beautiful wood panelling and glass interior of the building, the design inspired by the shape of a traditional Arabian dhow.

Baras not only starred, but also directed, staged and choreographed a show that paid tribute to six flamenco luminaries who had influenced her own work. Without knowing much about the other exponents she was indebted to, we no doubt missed the subtleties of the performance, but none of the passion and drama of seeing live flamenco performed by an artiste at the top of her game.

Most, though as Tim noticed, not all the music, was played live. Pre-recorded Spanish narrations introduced various sections of the show. It was a tall order to expect the audience to be fluent Spanish speakers and a little disappointing that a translation into Arabic and English couldn't be provided.

Baras led a company of fifteen performers, including the compelling José Serrano. Whilst much of the thrill of the show was created around intensity and speed, the moments of contrast and control displayed by the leading lady when making the barest contact with the floor was compelling to watch.

At the end of the night La Baras demanded that every corner of the house demonstrate its full and well-deserved appreciation. Watching her use her whole body to tell us what she expected us to do, namely applaud and with more, intensity, if you please, was a masterclass in the art of silent communication. Brava!

39

Dead Sea Healing

I'll always remember where I was when I heard that against all predictions, His Donald Trumpness – surely the joke candidate, was the new US President Elect. I woke up to this news on my second trip to Jordan when television pictures showed that even Mr Trump seemed slightly startled by the new reality. Much has happened since, not least his outrageous allegations of a "stolen" second term and the subsequent storming of the Capital building by his crazed supporters. As I recall, even before the vote that first put him in the White House, he had already talked about exposing what he believed would be a Hillary Clinton "rigged" win, but enough of him.

There was something else that was leaving me breathless with disbelief and causing my legs to fly out at unusual angles to boot. It was a dip in the Dead Sea.

On our first visit we'd been to the spectacular Petra site but couldn't fit a visit to the Dead Sea into the schedule. A return trip to Jordan was always planned. By lucky chance we'd arrived at the lowest point on earth, right at the end of the busy season when temperatures were perfect and visitor numbers low. The peacefulness of the area was immediately striking and welcome too, after the shock and awe of the news headlines.

The Dead Sea is a salt water lake, some four hundred metres below sea level and counting. The salt content is visible on the shoreline as sizeable, glittering crystals and its mineral-rich black mud is nature's very own spa treatment, said to improve circulation, soothe aches and pains and detox the skin. The idea was to slather it on face and body, let it form a crust on the skin for fifteen minutes and then wash it off in the waters. I didn't regret turning down the mud treatment, having seen others go for it. It was the healing waters I'd come for.

I'm not a confident swimmer and usually have to be cajoled to take a dip in the sea. Conditions have to feel right and even then I'm not too happy being out of my depth. Wading into unknown waters was therefore rare for me but this was different. I could see others floating on their backs and even though I was only in up to my waist, the water felt peculiar on my skin, syrupy and heavy.

I tentatively lifted a foot and, as if by magic, both legs shot from underneath me and I was afloat, bobbing on the water like a sea creature. It was a liberating, relaxing sensation and must be even more so for those with mobility issues. No fish can survive in the saltiness of the Dead Sea but humans in these waters with heads back, arms outstretched and straight legs resemble a new, crucifix-shaped species.

For maximum pleasure it was wise to abandon any thoughts of swimming on your front and to avoid splashing water in your eyes. Using my hands as crude paddles I could steer myself in any direction with ease. Touchdown on the sea bed was best accomplished in the shallows, using your hands to anchor yourself.

The mud treatment could be purchased in sachets for use at home, and while the commercial exploitation of this natural product was somewhat inevitable, the actual experience at the waterside was not prettified much beyond a towel and a shower. There was quite a bit of clambering down to the shoreline and I was glad to have had a heads up on the stony ground at the water's edge, so came prepared with waterproof beach shoes.

Across the water and beyond the Judaea mountains lie sacred and holy places, their names resonant with history, conflict and faith – Jerusalem, Jericho, the West Bank, Bethlehem and Hebron. Not far from where we were was the site where it is said that Jesus was baptised. No wonder it felt spiritual, the sort of place where miracles could happen.

The Dead Sea Panorama complex and museum was a short drive away. From a high look-out point in the early evening we enjoyed fabulous sunset views at the best time to capture the play of light on the water. The museum outlined the history, geology and the unique ecosystem of the area.

I'd read some bad reviews of bathing in the Dead Sea but I went back for more on another day. I suffered no stinging, itching or burning sensations, just silky smooth skin, with body and mind, floaty and relaxed. A perfect antidote to Donald's Trumpery.

40

Three Cities in Iran: Shiraz

It seemed as if it would never happen but finally, after all the official documents were in order, a six-night stay in Iran became a reality. Tim had been travelling from Dubai to Tehran for work quite regularly but this was our opportunity for a trip together. With a seven-day visa, we only had a couple of days in each city to access the history, heritage, beauty, and cultural achievements of this remarkable country. No problem. They are everywhere.

Thanks to our hosts we also had an insight into everyday life, and answers to our questions about the Iranian lifestyle. It is important to note, because it cannot be said often enough, that the government of Iran is different from the Iranian people. The amazing welcome and kindness from total strangers everywhere we went in Iran was in direct contrast to the received information, such as you find in the official advice to travellers on the UK government website. A section on safety and security reads: *"You should consider carefully the risks of travelling to Iran. If you choose to travel, you may wish to keep a low profile."*

Keeping a low profile is an interesting idea but it doesn't quite work in a place that is so friendly and where we were very obviously not locals. The average person on the street appeared delighted to see visitors from abroad and Iranians approached us, expressly to tell us so. The British are a rare breed in Iran and we had the impression our presence reminded the older generation of the times before the fall of the Shah.

No one we encountered appeared fearful of speaking to us and we felt safe to walk around and take photos wherever we went.

The welcome to Iran actually started on our flight out of Dubai when a charming young woman gave us a recommendation for eating out in Shiraz. It transpired that this was her home town and if we needed her help during our stay she was at our disposal. She was as good as her word and even texted the next day to see if we needed her assistance.

Once we'd checked in to our hotel, which was comfortable on the inside and with an impressive exterior, reminiscent of Thunderbird's Tracy Island, it was time to explore, starting with the famous Bazaar Vakil in the historic centre. Our attempts at correct Farsi pronunciation baffled our taxi driver but undeterred, he flagged down a passing pedestrian who could translate. Our first experience of a typical Iranian bazaar didn't disappoint. An enormous warren of passageways and courtyards, dating from the 1760s, with extraordinary, vaulted ceilings is home to sellers of just about everything – carpets, traditional homewares, crafts, clothing, hanks of wool, fancy materials, spices and foodstuffs of every kind.

We stopped at a small café in the bazaar to share a snack called *Dizi*. This is a lamb, chickpea, bean and vegetable stew with a twist. At the table, the strained stew arrived in a container with a mashing instrument attached. The cooking broth from the stew came in a separate bowl, along with a plate of warm flatbread. Using the masher, our server pressed the stew to a pulp. The idea was to use a piece of bread to pick up pieces of the mashed stew and then dip the bread into the broth. Exceptionally delicious.

The bazaar was quiet when we arrived but towards the end of the afternoon the passageways started to fill up and the traffic building up around the centre indicated locals were on a mission to shop.

Our arrival in Iran coincided with the run up to the Iranian New Year or *Nowruz*. Celebrations begin on 21 March and last for three weeks. In preparation for this special time of year women shop till they drop for new clothes and homewares. After a thorough spring clean, old household items are routinely replaced. Symbols of new life, including decorated eggs are all part of it too. It sounded very much like our own preparations for Christmas and Easter rolled into one giant festival and when I ventured to ask if women found this time of year a little stressful, the question was answered in the affirmative!

An interesting aspect to the Iranian New Year is the ritual of displaying seven items beginning with the letter S in homes and offices. These are: *Seeb* (apple), either *Serke* (vinegar) or a spice, (Sumac), *Sabze* (green grass), *Senjed* (a special kind of berry), *Samanoo* (a meal of wheat), *Sekke* (coin), and *Seer* (garlic).

On our first day in Shiraz we also explored the 18th century Karim Khan citadel and orange gardens. Amongst the most impressive features were the bathhouse, the stained glass windows and decorative wood surrounds. The heavens opened while we were there so we didn't linger for too long in the gardens. The orange fruits were visible though, the same variety grown in Seville, used to make marmalade. In Iran, this fruit is known as bitter orange or *narenj* and adds an extra depth of sharp, citrus flavour to soups, stews and dressings.

When the rain stopped we walked around the town, looking in the windows of the small shops selling pickles, and watching as freshly baked bread was put on display racks to cool. Beyond this we could see a crowd had gathered by a stand at the end of the street. As we neared we could see glasses of tea and pieces of cake were being handed out but no money appeared to be changing hands.

We hung back, unsure what was going on but were soon encouraged to come forward and join in. Free tea and cake? What a country! And it didn't stop there. We saw a helper carrying a tray to the road. As cars came to a stop at the traffic lights, windows were wound down and refreshments handed in.

It was only later that we found out this gesture was associated with a funeral or memorial service taking place at the nearby mosque. Traditionally, relatives of the deceased provide food and drink to all who pass by as a blessing.

Shiraz is renowned in Iran for the cultivation and celebration of the narcissus flower or *narges*. Later that evening, on our way to that recommended restaurant for dinner, we passed two young men, one of whom handed Tim a bunch of narcissus. No thank you, we said in our British way. They looked so hurt by our refusal to accept the flowers that we stopped. As it happened, this had been nothing more than a friendly, seasonal gesture.

One of the men spoke good English and explained the significance of the flowers. Sharing their exquisite perfume is said to make everyone happy. The pair then insisted on taking us to the restaurant we were looking for and even drove us to the door. What kindness!

Haft Khan is a complex with different dining options. We chose the traditional Iranian restaurant and it was so good we went back the next night. They made a point of asking visitors what country they were from. The flag representing the foreign country, together with the Iranian flag were displayed on the table together. This restaurant had a vast collection of flags and I noticed this at other places too. Another sign of friendship and welcome, flying in the face of the UK government's grim advice to travellers.

The food was fantastic. We particularly enjoyed the appetiser of soft cheese with crushed walnuts which we spread onto warm flat bread. The Iranians love fresh herbs and a basket of chives, chervil and mint invited each person to choose their preferred garnish. Savoury sauces, sweetened with pomegranate molasses featured here and rice was elevated to new heights, either crispy-topped and fragrant with saffron or studded with tiny, crimson, slightly sour barberries. Just what you needed to soak up a plentiful, tasty sauce. We shared a dish of roasted baby chicken with plums, walnuts, raisins, almonds and pistachios and also tried a hearty stew of lamb, split peas and aubergine. The latter had a satisfying citrus kick with the addition of dried black lime. It was all faultless and very satisfying after a day of sightseeing.

After asking where are you from, the second most asked question of any visitor to Shiraz is, how are you getting to Persepolis?' At just an hour's drive away, it is inconceivable that anyone would come to Shiraz without including the vast World

Heritage site and spectacular ruins of the mighty Achaemenid Empire on their itinerary.

The great symbol of Persian civilisation and power took more than fifty years to build. When Alexander the Great conquered the Persian capital city in 330 BC he looted its treasures and set fire to the city. The ruins of the former royal palaces, gates, great halls, tombs, and the decorative reliefs that remain, are testament to the might and ambition of Darius the Great and his son Xerxes.

Our tour guide provided us with enough of the historical background and details we needed to appreciate it on a single visit, and we felt privileged to have access to such a precious piece of the ancient past. The scale and sophistication of the structure is remarkable and on our visit crowds of Iranian photography students were also aiming to capture images of one of the world's great archaeological sites.

We returned to Shiraz in the afternoon to wander through the peaceful, landscaped historic Eram Garden and then to visit the tomb of the adored 14th century Persian poet, Havez. Our first two days in Iran had been steeped in culture. Next stop, Isfahan.

41

Three Cities in Iran: Isfahan

The journey north from Shiraz to Isfahan is a five-hour drive, covering three hundred miles, so we made an early appearance at Shiraz bus station. Isfahan is the ancient former capital of Persia, renowned for its historic sites, art and Islamic architecture.

Thanks to a helpful taxi driver we joined the right queue for our intended destination. After close examination of our paperwork we were issued with a flimsy sheet of paper that said we could climb aboard.

It was Tim's birthday so we planned to search for cake when we arrived. With palaces, bridges, gardens, cathedrals, bazaars, museums and paintings to see, we would barely have time to scratch the surface of Isfahan's treasures in two days. To help us make the most of the short time we had, our hosts had arranged a half-day tour of some of the key attractions for the next morning. Meanwhile we headed straight for Isfahan's main attraction, the magnificent Naghsh-e Jahan Square.

One of the largest city squares in the world, is in fact a long rectangle with masterpieces of Islamic architecture in every direction. In past times the area was a polo field, which is some indication of its scale. The Persians invented the game of polo and much else, including the exchange of goods through a monetary system, a postal service and the first human rights charter. Religious tolerance is still part of Iranian culture so churches, cathedrals and synagogues, as well as mosques, are evident in Isfahan and other Iranian cities. I wouldn't have believed it before coming here, which just goes to show that the narrative we are fed about Iran in the West is in sharp contrast to the cultural norms of the country.

Naghsh-e Jahan Square may be another World Heritage site but what was most striking is the key role it has today in all aspects of local life. Families and the young gather here by day and evening to enjoy a walk, to shop and to socialise. The equine heritage is a little more sedate now than on the original polo field as these days, attractive horse-drawn carriages ferry visitors around. With leisure, pleasure, commerce and worship all in the same area it was the perfect place to experience the spirit of Isfahan when time was so brief.

I couldn't imagine ever becoming tired or over familiar with the nooks and crannies of the bazaar located in and around the square's edge. Duck into any opening and the vast labyrinth of passageways and courtyards, crammed with stalls, shops and tea houses revealed a shopper's paradise. Beautifully crafted items I didn't realise I needed were on show in every direction. Handicrafts, jewellery, ceramics, homewares, in silver filigree and copper, colourful textiles and of course, exquisite rugs and carpets, unique to this region. I made a mental note to return to the shopping area the next day. In the meantime, where could we eat? There was a birthday to celebrate.

An online search for restaurants highlighted *Shahrzad* and it was a short walk from our hotel. The reviews said it was popular and sure enough the upstairs dining room started to fill up with locals soon after we arrived. Apart from the sugar content,

Iranian food is generally healthy and wholesome. A plate of varied salad vegetables is a standard first course. Tim ordered lamb chops and I tried *Khoresh Fesenjan,* an Iranian speciality of chicken, stewed in a sauce of walnut and pomegranate molasses. All the food was very tasty and portions huge, though not especially pretty on the plate.

Tahdig, the crispy topped rice we'd had in Shiraz wasn't such a feature on menus in Isfahan. White rice topped with a little saffron or sometimes studded with little red barberries was more usual. Officially, no alcohol was available in Iran so non-alcoholic drinks, such as "lemon beer," were served in restaurants. The bottle and label design suggested beer but the drink tasted pretty much like lemonade. We took to the culture of Iranian teahouses though and enjoyed the black tea with lemon verbena at one in particular. Tea was served with a pretty dipping stick of saffron sugar crystals balanced on the saucer.

We found the citizens of Isfahan just as friendly as those we encountered in Shiraz. Window shopping, we were approached by a local guy who told us he taught English and was keen to have a conversation with native speakers. Could he show us a place that served cake? No problem. We chatted over coffee and slices of standard cake at his favourite, but disappointingly westernised café. He turned out to be a huge fan of the singer, Adele and assumed we would know the answers to the questions he posed about her personal life. In spite of our lack of useful intel he very kindly invited us to join his family for lunch the next day, but we told him we'd be on a tour. He mentioned that his relatives had a carpet shop close to the Armenian Cathedral. This didn't mean too much at the time.

The next morning our guide took us back to Naqsh-i Jahan Square to walk amongst the stunning blue and turquoise tiles and mosaics inside the Sheikh Lotfollah Mosque. We stopped for a drink in the nearby park, before entering the Chehel Sotoun pavilion, standing at the far end of a long water pool, Inside, we walked through rooms of magnificent paintings and frescoes in stunning colours, depicting ancient Persian stories. Chehel Sotoun literally means, "forty columns" because the wooden structures supporting the entrance appear to number forty in the water's reflection.

By amazing coincidence, our tour concluded near a carpet shop by the magnificent Vank Cathedral. Curious, we went in and an assistant immediately asked us if Tim had celebrated a birthday the previous day. Our cake companion was his cousin and word had been passed to look after two Brits, should they happen to drop in. We were treated to a fascinating presentation on Persian carpets and patterns, thinly disguised as a charming sales pitch. It worked. No regrets!

Later, we made a point of trying a couple of local specialities that we'd heard about. *Beryouni* is a fried minced lamb patty, wrapped in bread and served with a yoghurt sauce. A tasty morsel that Tim thought achieved a depth of flavour only possible with the addition of offal. I found out that later that lungs were probably in the mix. I'm glad we didn't know that at the time.

The Iranians love sweet tastes and especially nougat, which they call *Gaz*. We noticed shops dedicated to this and similar products. In the *Azadegan Café*, a traditional haunt, with dusty bric-a-brac adorning every spare inch of the ceiling and walls, a plate of sticky shapes called *bamiyeh* are served with tea. These are made from deep-fried dough, dipped in syrup. Toothachingly sweet!

Vivid colours and patterns were not confined to the mosques and palaces. We stayed at the famous Abassi hotel, a complex built at the time of King Sultan Husayn, three hundred years ago, and restored in the 1950s. Here too, a grand outdoor courtyard and Iranian decorative features, steeped in history, added to our experience of Isfahan.

A short domestic flight north brought us to our third and final stop, Tehran.

42

Three Cities In Iran: Tehran

Tehran, the capital city, is a sprawling metropolis of eight million where thanks to our hosts we experienced a little of everyday life in Iran. Our friends and their dear little boy were our guides. Then aged four, he was a fan of the children's characters Topsy and Tim and was delighted to meet a real life Tim. That made me Topsy. Even though we didn't seem to behave much like the story book people, he seemed happy enough to share his mum and dad with us for a couple of days.

We'd arrived on the anniversary of the death of the prophet's daughter, Fatima and noted the black flags displayed on public buildings as we left Isfahan. In Tehran, evening prayers were taking place at a shrine close to a local bazaar.

As we walked through the bazaar, our host explained that everyone shopped here, rich and poor alike. The bazaar was a great leveller. I could see why. It was a cook's paradise, with fresh fruit, vegetables and cookware at every turn. The sacks of tantalising spices, teas, dried fruits and nuts looked so attractive that we were easily persuaded to make several purchases. At one stand they were cooking fresh baby beetroots and selling them like kebabs on a stick. Just my kind of street food.

I'd developed a taste for saffron on this trip. Iranian saffron is the best in the world and just a few of the tiny red filaments brings a vivid yellow colour to rice or plain yoghurt, and a pleasing floral flavour. The highly prized spice used to flavour and colour food has health benefits too, but I hadn't fully appreciated the taste because the quality you find on the average UK supermarket shelf is inferior in comparison. With top quality Iranian saffron, it was worth investing in a handy little gadget on sale in the bazaar. Every Iranian home has a saffron grinder to reduce the precious filaments to a fine powder, thus making the spice go even further. Sold!

Luxury items, as well as provisions were available in the bazaar too. From Shiraz, I took home a silver filigree necklace with a central stone of lapis lazuli. From Tehran, I'll treasure a beautiful turquoise and silver bracelet, a gift from our generous hosts.

Iranian culture places guests at VIP level and the generosity shown to visitors to the country is so touching. Here's one example. Our hosts took me to an exhibition and sale of decorative homewares. This was well-timed to coincide with preparations for the Iranian New Year when purchasing fashionable items for the home is part of the celebration. Unlike the bazaar, this had a definite air of exclusivity about it. The venue, in the middle of a public garden, had attracted a privileged class of beautiful, well-dressed women. I hadn't planned to buy anything but it was interesting to browse as there were some gorgeous pieces. The framed pictures and furniture on display were obviously too large and fragile to consider, but a small metal bowl lined with bright blue enamel was begging for attention. I could find a space for that in my suitcase.

Paying for anything in Iran is a little complicated as there are two currencies, the rial and the toman. American dollars are also acceptable in some situations and it was these, and only these that I had in my purse. This was effectively a pop-up shop and the sales assistant was not set up for US dollars but she had a solution. 'You're a guest here, take it as a gift, from us,' she said with a smile, 'Look I will make a note right here on my list that we are giving you a present.' She even wrapped it for me. Would this happen anywhere in Europe? I don't think so. Utterly charming.

Also located in the garden is the Museum of Time. The building, with its ornate architecture and decorative mouldings was as fascinating as the collections of historic clocks and watches it houses. On the top floor, quirky modern artwork using watch parts to create imagery offered a neat contrast.

While we were exploring the treasures in the garden Tim had been taken by car to snow covered slopes for a cable car ride, all just twenty minutes away from the city.

After all that activity we went for lunch at the wonderful *Narenjestan*, a restaurant listed in Tehran's top ten. The dining area offered a magnificent view of the city but it was the five star standard of food and service that made it special. Our waiter, educated in London years ago spoke impeccable English.

The menu featured Persian, international and seafood dishes, and everything we ordered was first class in presentation and taste. Live classical music was playing too. A memorable conclusion to our six days.

Iran is a country that can't fail to impress and our experience exceeded all expectations. The warmth and generosity of the people, the incredible history, art and culture is truly enriching.

We can only hope for better understanding between our governments in the future.

What about the mandatory headscarf? Was it a problem? By law, all women, must cover their hair in public in Iran, including tourists. It's controversial and I didn't much like it. Two out of three Iranian women I asked agreed with me. That said, I saw so many women who really rocked the look in a way that almost made me envious. Younger women wore the headscarf as far back as they dared and there were of course, designer versions with colour and pattern to add glamour and chic to the look. Women will always find a way to show individual style and personality, whatever the rules!

43

It's Showtime!

Short+Sweet is the largest festival of ten-minute plays in the world and the Dubai event is a landmark in the theatrical calendar. Over six weeks, talented writers, directors, and actors present around eighty short plays to packed houses and acclaim.

It's an annual vehicle for just about any and every theatrical form and topic but it is also a competition that everyone wants to win.

An audition process puts actors in front of directors months ahead of the performance dates, but a considerable proportion of the plays are cast at a scarily late stage. There are a lot of distractions in Dubai, which can be problematic as it requires a degree of staying power to see something like this through from start to finish. From time to time many employees need to travel internationally so work life isn't always compatible with a strict rehearsal schedule. Traffic on the key routes also conspires against anyone being able to get across town by a set time. Even if the roads are clear, taxi drivers may not be familiar with the rehearsal address.

As the plays are only ten minutes long every second counts as far as the script and characterisations go. It has to be slick, concise and clear from the get go and the biggest danger is running over time. A second over the allotted ten minutes means instant disqualification. Scripts may have to be ruthlessly cut and business perfected on the hoof, often in less than ideal rehearsal spaces. The number of opportunities left to get it right before performance day soon evaporates to single figures.

Exactly a year since we started our expat adventure in Dubai, and in keeping with my general aim of making the most of this fast-moving experience, I made my stage debut at the *Short+ Sweet Festival of Theatre 2016.* The play, titled *Ladies Night,* took a wry look at how the rituals of a typical club night in Dubai makes fools of the women that attend them. Research for the role involved going to one of these notorious events. I learned a lot. Mainly, that the reason single women consumed the copious quantities of free champagne laid on at these club nights was to convince themselves and everyone else that they were having a good time.

It was a good topic but somehow failed to connect with the audience. We got knocked out in the first round. Next time I planned to have a go at writing my own material.

Several months later I signed up for a weekend course to learn the basics of ten-minute playwriting from a locally based master in the art of writing short plays. A bunch of us wannabe playwrights were schooled in how to craft a suitably theatrical script, devise great dialogue and create memorable characters. Armed with this knowledge we were charged to return the next day with copies of our freshly created play. A group of volunteer actors had been called in to help workshop our first drafts, thus road-testing their entertainment value.

It all appeared straightforward enough but later that night, a plateful of biscuits within reach, I found myself staring at a blank screen, waiting for inspiration to strike. During the day everyone else on the course had outlined straightforward ideas that would easily translate to the stage. I had one idea that I kept coming back to but it was complicated. The golden rule for a ten-minute play was to keep it simple and clear and my idea was hardly that. I wanted to write about an actor and the process of acting. My story centred around a troubled thespian named Mike who confesses a secret to the audience. I fancied the idea of breaking the fourth wall and having Mike share something with the audience about his real life that mirrored his stage life. I love black comedy so I was aiming to make the script darkly funny, entertaining and at the same time, intriguing.

If I pulled it off, the audience would be watching a play, a rehearsal of a play and a comic crime scene. All at the same time, and in ten minutes. The only person not in on my leading actor's audacious act of revenge against an indiscreet co-star would be their gullible director, who would be duped into thinking that both actors were giving the performance of their lives. The working title was *Just Playing* and it was absurdly ambitious.

Working late into the night I eventually had the barest outline, and in the workshop the next day the feedback led me to believe it had potential. The plan was to improve the script and submit it for *Short+Sweet 2017*. The competition is open to three groups of people. Writers submit their plays, directors choose the scripts they want to work on and then select the cast from a pool of interested actors. A certain amount of overlap is permitted as a writer of one play could be directing their own and acting in another.

Unless you're a tried and tested *Short+Sweet* playwright, or the equivalent of Neil Simon, the chances of a director picking your random idea and running with it are not exactly zero, but pretty close. The advice to writers was to direct your own play but not to try acting in it as well. All I needed was four willing actors. Should be easy enough in a theatre scene as lively as Dubai, with so much talent? Yes, and no.

Naturally, every director wants to entice the best actors to be in their play and competition is fierce when it comes to casting. I had a background in theatre but no history of success in Dubai so no one was going to be beating a path to my door anytime soon. Directors can also cast from open auditions and this was where my *Short+Sweet* journey started to get interesting. I was scouting around for actors around October for a ten-minute performance to be staged the following February, and it wasn't a minute too soon. For a start, one of the parts was mostly mime. Not a very appealing prospect for most actors who generally value quantity of dialogue over meaningful silence.

At the auditions, attended by at least twenty other directors, I picked out potential candidates, noted down their details and made contact. Every other director was doing the same thing and all this attention and demand definitely goes to some actor's heads. It turned casting a play into an experience akin to speed dating. In the communications that followed it seemed the actors needed to audition me before committing themselves. One even sent me an outrageously rude reply after I emailed him the script! Whoa! Who asked you for a review? No thanks would do!

Others who had tried out for a role in full knowledge of the performance dates, decided they weren't available after all or, more likely, were reluctant to commit in case a better offer came along a little later. Annoying. Suddenly this *Short+Sweet* thing all seemed a bit too difficult, but as I found out later this was a pretty standard experience. It was a competition after all and everyone wanted to give themselves the best possible chance of success. In the end, and before I lost my nerve altogether, I asked around for acting recommendations and used social media to advertise my requirements. Finally, my cast was complete. For a while.

Working life in Dubai is demanding with long hours and unpredictable schedules the norm. My leading actor was rock solid from day one but gathering all the other cast members together at the same time, for more than two consecutive rehearsals was like herding cats.

Throw in the Dubai traffic and the impossibility of arriving anywhere on time and the schedule soon went out of the window. Meanwhile the performance dates were in sight. Despite everyone's best intentions or expectations two of my four actors had to drop out and the co-star's ego prevented him from turning up to rehearsals. What a casting disaster that was! Fortunately, part of the solution was in plain sight.

Who will always turn up to rehearsal? Who will be supportive and helpful at all times? Who could actually do this quite well? Who will be happy to take direction and who needs a challenge and some fun, outside of work? Tim!

ME: OK, I think you could do this. It's a bit of mime and just three lines of dialogue at the end.

TIM: Are you out of your mind? I've never acted in my life.

ME: I know, but there's nothing to it, really. I'll coach you. In fact, I'm going to be in it too now! Not ideal I know, but the only female role needs to be filled as well and it's easier if I just do it myself at this stage.

TIM: I'm really worried about the lines.

ME: No need. Don't panic about the lines! The miming and acting dead you'll have to do is much more difficult!

TIM: Whaaaaat?

I'd already found an excellent replacement for the co-star role and my script had started to spring to life in rehearsals. I felt sure the performance could fulfil its promise to amuse and entertain with both of us playing the remaining parts. We all pressed on with rehearsals and soon started to get excited about putting it in front of an audience.

Plays by first-time writers, or simply because the content is unusual, are generally programmed in the Wildcards section of *Short+Sweet* and many get knocked out in the first round, so we were all thrilled when *Just Playing* was voted through to the next stage. This meant we presented it twice and only very narrowly missed out on a place in the Gala Finals. There were plenty of laughs and some terrific feedback from audiences and judges after both shows. Success beyond anyone's dreams.

The verdict from Tim, the erstwhile non-actor among us, after making a highly effective stage debut, was that he'd love to do it all over again because it was so enjoyable. He channelled his inner Marcel Marceau to perfection and all things considered, our experience proved that there's more to winning than coming first.

44

Georgia on my Mind

I doubt Georgia would ever have been on my holiday radar in the UK, but the world map looked so different from Dubai. The capital, Tbilisi, was just a three-hour flight away. Georgia lies to the south of Russia, where Eastern Europe meets Asia.

Black Sea beaches, beautiful countryside, mountains, caves, fortresses, monasteries and one of the oldest wine-producing regions in the world, make Georgia well worth exploring. The country's history has been turbulent, with independence from the Soviet Union finally won in 1991. Perhaps for this reason, pride in the traditions and heritage of the country is tangible and Georgians love to celebrate their cultural identity in music. Every evening of our trip, we came across groups of musician in bars and cafés across the city, entertaining locals and visitors with traditional Georgian songs.

In the Old Town area of Tbilisi we found a mix of lively bars and restaurants, restored old buildings, historic monuments and striking contemporary architecture, notably the magnificent Peace Bridge. Carved wooden balconies gave the residential buildings vintage character and even the decaying examples had a photogenic grandeur to them.

Tbilisi literally means "heat" and refers to the city's naturally warm sulphur waters. A complex of domed bathhouses looked to be in the process of restoration and in the same area we spotted what we thought was an Iranian mosque. Later we learned that this too was a bathhouse, not yet open to the public, due to ongoing restoration work but deliberately fashioned in the distinctive Iranian style with decorative blue and turquoise tiles.

Up the side streets and alleyways leading away from the main thoroughfare, most of the buildings were in various stages of disrepair, some being held in place with metal supports. Families still lived in these buildings and judging from the piles of rubble it seemed to be a hazardous existence. Hopefully, the regeneration of the Old Town will soon extend to these areas.

It was in this unlikely setting that we happened upon the *Culinarium Cookery School*. As luck would have it the School's proprietors were taste-testing cakes from a local patisserie as we stumbled in. With tea supplied, we were invited to give our opinion on the products. It was hard to imagine a better welcome to a country, even if the cakes were a little garish and overly sweet for our taste.

The husband and wife managers of the cookery school told us they were food consultants to many of the city's food producers and restaurateurs. With so much local knowledge they were more than happy to give us a top tip on where to go for dinner. They even helped us secure a coveted table at *Barbarestan*, one of the best restaurants in the city. The menu, based entirely on a 19th century Georgian recipe book, found at a flea market certainly sounded intriguing. As a restaurant concept, it could have been style over substance but the excellence of the food expelled any doubts.

Cold vegetable starters included an aubergine and garlic dip and a dish of thinly sliced courgettes, covered with *satsivi,* a cold walnut sauce. Delicious, lightly toasted flatbread complemented them both. Perfectly pink duck with stewed pears, and a chicken and aubergine dish followed. The classic style, local red wine suggested by our server was among the best we tasted on this trip.

With time of the essence, the next morning we joined a free walking tour around Tbilisi's main attractions and the city's ancient Georgian orthodox churches. Georgians are deeply religious and the churches we visited were crowded with local worshippers.

Our American guide explained that the widespread corruption of the past had now been reversed. Prime Minister Giorgi Kvirikashvili, previously the leader of the Georgian Dream coalition, won an overwhelming majority at the last election, in what appeared to be a highly significant and positive result. Given the dire state of UK and US politics, I envied Georgia's sense of optimism. Imagine having an inspirational leader, with a mandate for a peaceful reboot of the country. If only.

Watching over the city's fortunes, and visible from our hotel room, was the statue of Mother Georgia, a twenty-metre high aluminium figure, representing the Georgian national character. In her left hand she holds a bowl of wine for those who come in friendship and in her right, a sword to deter enemies. Our guide took us up the hill on foot for a statue's eye view across the city. Cable cars ferry visitors up and down Sololaki Hill all day long to explore the various monuments and viewing points. With eyes shut throughout I could tolerate the descent without a panic attack. Cable cars are just not my thing.

We'd noticed lots of intriguing edibles on our wanderings and our guide had given us a few pointers on some typical local food to try. Stalls selling *churchkhela* were everywhere. Georgia's most popular sweet snack is made from thickened, concentrated grape juice and walnuts and on display looked like a rainbow of hanging sausages. It looked better than it tasted, though we avoided the highly coloured versions. True *churchkhela* should be the same colour as the red or white wine that is the main ingredient. Gaudy blues and greens were clearly pumped full of artificial colouring.

The most sophisticated interpretation of *churchkhela* we had was the dessert at *Barbarestan* where the red grape juice appeared as a lightly set jelly on a base of crushed walnuts, finished with a caramel sauce. Oh yes.

Georgians love walnuts and aubergines and make use of them in unusual ways. Walnut oil replaces olive as a dipping accompaniment to bread. Finely ground nuts might be sprinkled on top of a fresh tomato and cucumber salad and can also be added to *chakapuli,* a hearty meat stew. There's various versions of this, depending on the season. In the summer, the sauce might include sour plums and chunks of aubergine. It reminded me of dishes I'd eaten in Iran. Georgian cuisine has its own traditions but the spicing and ingredients favoured by invaders and traders over centuries has left its mark too.

As a wine-producing country of note, Georgia's drinking culture is huge and local wine shops are everywhere. Coming from the Middle East it was a bit weird to see encouraging slogans outside restaurants and bars, suggesting that wine consumption was the solution to most problems. Despite this we didn't see any evidence of drunken behaviour anywhere.

At a wine bar we ordered the Georgian tapas menu, as a way of sharing a selection of dishes in one sitting without being overstuffed. Our helpful waitress gave a useful explanation of the two types of Georgian wine. In brief, the classic style comprises reds and whites, made with Georgian grape varieties in the European tradition of winemaking. By contrast, traditional *qvevri* wines develop in earthenware pots and these are stored underground during the fermentation process. Grapes, skins, seeds and even the stalks go in. In a tasting of *quevri* wines we found them too dry to be enjoyable so we stuck to the classic style.

To accompany the wine, we chose *kupati*, a spicy Georgian sausage, served with a plum sauce and buttery mash. The sausage filling was course cut and probably contained bits of pig that we wouldn't have chosen to eat but the peppery spices worked their magic. Just as welcome was the little dish of beef and pork meatballs, fragrant with rosemary, and made even better with a spicy tomato dipping sauce.

Our appetiser of bread and walnut oil had satisfied the carb craving, so the dish of fried potatoes that came after the sausage and mash was barely touched. We were full after four dishes but the menu said five, and an enormous *khatchapuri* bread, stuffed with melted cheese completed our order. The Georgian equivalent of an after dinner mint. We got off lightly as it can arrive with a fried egg on top. We didn't have the heart to leave it completely untouched, so a good half was hastily torn off and hidden in my bag so it looked like we'd had a fair go at it. Travellers prone to indigestion, beware!

On our last full day we took a tour through the spectacular Georgian countryside. Tours on a mini bus with a driver and a guide were easy to find and inexpensive. Our tour took in several beauty spots and sites of religious significance as well as a wine-tasting and tour of the Khareba winery. The Bodbe monastery site was particularly serene and well cared for as it houses the resting place of St. Nino, a revered female figure in the early history of Christianity.

Our final destination, was Sighnaghi, named "city of love" because the registry office is always open and couples can get married without having to first file official documents. The Georgian equivalent of Gretna Green. Sighnaghi is on a hill and the steep climb up to the viewing point came right at the end of a full day's sightseeing, but was well worth the effort for the view across the rooftops.

45

Bye, Dubai

By July, 2017 our Dubai adventure was coming to a close and in the flurry of list-making, packing, re-packing, administration and goodbyes, there was time for a little reflection.

We'd been privileged guest residents in the UAE and made friends with others from around the world, though sadly, not a single native Emirati. It's hard to develop friendships with Emiratis outside the workplace or religious setting.

After two and half years away it felt good to be going home and starting afresh. I used to be afraid of momentous changes. Not anymore. Moving from everything and everyone I knew was daunting in February, 2015. Now it felt thrilling. Of the friends we'd made in Dubai, many had been expats somewhere all their working lives and their positive attitude about living in other countries had rubbed off.

We knew we wouldn't be expats again but we would always want to be travellers. Retirement had been the elephant in the room, looming large over our Dubai experience. We came to Dubai knowing that this would be the last assignment for Tim after nearly thirty years with the same company.

The concept of retirement is so loaded. Why does retiring from work automatically imply that you also retire from life? As the date for Tim to leave drew nearer many appeared concerned, disbelieving, even.

'What will you do?' was the usual response, as if without daily paid employment, the unfortunate retiree will be compelled to gaze around their surroundings in bewilderment. The same question, posed so many times can become a self-fulfilling and paralysing prophecy. After looking forward to exploring new opportunities, and having the freedom to do so, even Tim started to have misgivings.

A wobble or two was understandable. There was the official handover and goodbye celebrations with colleagues and the touching and kind messages. One day you've got a role and a title, you put on your office attire, leave the house at 8.30am and the next day you don't. Or the next day, or the day after that.

The reality of leaving work didn't sink in immediately and for many months Tim remained in the fuzzy no man's land of employment limbo. Mentally, neither totally in, nor completely out. A helpful transition.

Managing a permanent gap year requires structure and disruption. If retirement looms and you're seeking ideas on how to make it work for you, read on!

1. Physically leave your comfort zone.

Research a different country, pack your bags, put your extra stuff in storage and live a different life for a while. Rent your home or arrange a house swap. This was part of our pre-Covid plan and might still be on the cards one day.

2. Mentally leave your comfort zone.

Set yourself a challenge. Draft a book, design an app or enrol on a course. Whatever you choose to do, connect with the like-minded, both in person and through free, online platforms. Seek out the social media groups that foster mutual encouragement and positive feedback.

3. Be acutely aware of time.

When you have an abundance of free time there's a tendency to waste it. Everyone needs a period to just chill and do nothing occasionally, but once you've embarked on a project you need to stay interested to see it through. Interest and motivation comes from doing, not just thinking about doing. Set yourself a realistic schedule that you can stick to and milestones you can achieve daily, over a month, three months, six months.

4. Sell or refurbish?

Look at your home. Imagine if you had to either sell it or alter it. What would you choose to do? Look into the possibilities of both. Discuss ideas and costs. How does an extension stack up against selling and buying somewhere else? It's an interesting exercise and can throw up some surprising results. We thought we wanted to refurbish but after considering the plans, costs and likely results, changed our minds.

5. Refurbishing your home.

What are the priorities? It's easy to get carried away with refurbishment, especially if an enthusiastic and creative architect outlines ambitious plans. Knock this wall down here, open this room up there, transform that empty loft space with a super-duper conversion. All great, but if all you really want is a bigger kitchen, and none of the ideas address that, then refurbishment could be very costly and time-consuming. We concluded we just didn't have the stomach, and possibly the heart to stay on top of a major project. We had an early warning sign of how it might go, so I pass this on in case it's helpful. If builders struggle to get back to you with a straightforward price in a reasonable period of time, it tells you they could be equally unreliable if hired.

Going over budget might cause nothing more than a raised eyebrow to camera on a television programme, but if that's *your* money disappearing in extended schedules and unexpected price hikes you might wish you hadn't started. We took the hint.

6. Selling your home.

Before we came to Dubai we'd lived in the same house for twenty-three years. We'd brought up our children in that house and gradually altered and arranged it to suit our needs as the years went by. We knew the history of all its special peculiarities and comforts. There was nothing we didn't know about that house. Both our sons had left home and hadn't looked back. It was time for us to say goodbye and move on too. If we loved the house, others would too. We'd rented it out whilst we were in Dubai and after that it didn't feel like our home any more. Returning to the same old, same old just wasn't for us. A new home awaited us somewhere, and with a permanent gap year to fill we had plenty of time to find it.

46

Location, Location, Location

Following two and half years in the adult playground-cum-sandpit of Dubai we returned to the motherland in September 2017, free as birds. We could live anywhere in the UK, but where to look? Yorkshire was our beautiful home county for many years but we fancied a change, and a kinder climate because after Dubai, severe, north of England winters had lost their appeal. Many viewings later, across several southern counties, we found The One.

Our new and permanent home, sits on the rural borderlands of Essex and Suffolk. The house is in Essex but down the road the signs announce a welcome to Suffolk. Landscapes and views that inspired Constable and Gainsborough are all around us.

'You've chosen well, here – gorgeous spot and the driest place in England, this is,' was the message from the array of tradesmen with either Essex or Suffolk accents that arrived at our door in the first month.

The south-facing garden, predicted by the same to be as hot as a Spanish holiday resort come spring, remained stubbornly uninviting. Initially, we endured freezing temperatures and unprecedented amounts of snow, followed by gales, driving rain and hail.

In truth we didn't exactly choose the place, we chose the house, but when the sun did eventually break through, our hunches were right. There was a lot to love. First off, fresh food markets and farm shops were the norm. Finally, growing, buying, cooking and eating fresh local produce was not aspirational, it's just what everyone did. Gussied up food emporiums could be found in these parts and they certainly had their place but so did the fresh fish van, with a chalkboard boasting the day's bargain catch, the village shop selling produce from the nearest farm, and neighbours that looked to share the fruit and veg glut of the season from their own gardens and plots.

Lots of villagers roundabout keep chickens, box up the eggs and offer them for sale outside their homes. A modest payment is left on trust. On most weekends smallholders and artisan producers selling veg, rapeseed oil, and even spirits can be found on a village green or farmer's market somewhere nearby.

Our neighbours have been so welcoming. The removal van advertising our arrival, effectively blocked the lane for two days but no one seemed too bothered. A steady stream of kind-hearted souls, bearing cards and gifts introduced themselves, always ready to answer our endless queries about the recycling system and much else that us townies found mysterious about living in the country during those first weeks of snow and ice.

We had some misgivings about moving to a rural location without the conveniences of a town or city close at hand. No one could have predicted that a home and garden in peaceful countryside might be the best place to be in the event of a pandemic. At this point, Covid-19 was still two years away,

London just a short train ride from home, and the Rolling Stones were coming to town.

47

London Calling:
The Rolling Stones May 2018

Charles Robert Watts (2 June 1941 – 24 August 2021).

Sadly, the death of the legendary drummer, Charlie Watts was announced as I was putting this collection together. He was eighty years old and had been a member of the Rolling Stones since 1963.

Business and pleasure only took us back to the capital for two or three nights but it turns out we were missed in our village, as on our return our neighbours declared it was good to see us back. In London, where we were insignificant specks in the crowd it felt good that someone at home noticed our absence.

The lure of the capital city is undeniable though, and we had planned this trip around seeing the Rolling Stones concert at London Stadium in the Olympic Park. Aside from the main event, with a little research we enjoyed one of the best free experiences the city has to offer. Sky Garden on the 35th floor of the so-called Walkie Talkie building in Fenchurch Street offers access to London's highest public garden, and panoramic views across the city from the observation decks. It's necessary to book ahead for tickets but we got lucky and thanks to a cancellation were able to bag a couple on the day.

After taking in the stunning free views we strolled through landscaped terraces of abundant and lush flowering plants, ferns, grasses and herbs. Suitably impressed, we were ready to empty our wallets at one of several bars and restaurants. As the day was young and we really know how to live, we settled on a couple of non-alcoholic cocktails and a packet of crisps, waving goodbye to the best part of twenty pounds in the process. A snip though, compared to anything similar in Dubai, where they know a thing or two about iconic buildings and persuading vast numbers to part with wads of cash to see them.

The evening before we'd enjoyed an excellent dinner in Islington with friends who live in the area. They introduced us to the French bistro *La Petite Auberge*, one of their favourites amongst many in lively Upper Street. Our mains were signature French. A heavenly Boeuf Bourguignon – the ultimate melt in the mouth slow food, with a rich red wine sauce and a pile of fluffy mash to soak it up. Even a humble chicken breast, generously stuffed with spinach and ricotta cheese was turned into an extra special dish with the addition of a creamy sauce, richly flavoured with earthy mushrooms and chicken juices. Every ingredient tasted as if the maximum flavour had been squeezed out of it before chef added the obligatory half a pound of butter. Butter, cream, salt, and sugar, and plenty of them. It's no mystery why French food tastes so good!

It's not often that a traditional menu item makes me rethink a dish I know and love. Crème brûlée with banana? A crust of shiny brown caramel clinging to slices of banana atop a velvety, just set custard. Genius. The sort of dessert I dream about.

From the best dessert in the world to a bit of a flop. A restaurant with the heritage of the *German Gymnasium* should be able to produce the ultimate Black Forest gateau. Sadly not. This one had so much cream I wondered if chef was having a White Forest laugh. Not nearly enough chocolate in the sponge and the essential juicy cherry content squashed into a peculiar hard base. The whole thing was drenched in Amaretto, giving it a stridently almond flavour. Weird.

For those who care about these things the best Black Forest gateau in London can be found at *The Wolseley*. I nearly cried with joy when I ate it.

That said, the *German Gymnasium* at Kings Cross does a lot of things very well. The menu is a veritable meat fest and they do the sausage and schnitzel stuff to perfection. No complaints on the triple cooked chips either and the surroundings, general buzz and service is excellent too. I'd go back but pass on dessert.

Onto the main event. We were part of the standing crowd at the Olympic Park, waiting for the greatest rock and roll band in the world to show us what they still had. Good fortune again as the support act was Florence and the Machine (night one got Liam Gallagher). Flo, as she is known on Twitter, was outstanding, with great presence, lean, lithe and charmingly humble, she delivered a clutch of crowd-pleasing hits, but no one was screaming for an encore for obvious reasons.

A brief pause before the lights, the guitar riff, and a roar of approval from the crowd. Jumpin' Jack Flash and his trusty musical lieutenants were off, and all my black and white yesterdays were playing back to me in glorious colour. If it felt like that for me, what did it feel like for them?

Every minute of the sex, drugs, rock and roll royalty lifestyle is etched deep into those crumbling faces. The peerless, legendary hits they played were the soundtrack to their lives too. Longevity has made the Rolling Stones their own tribute to their youth and ours.

As they went into *Let's Spend the Night Together* I could still hear my parents' outrage at the sentiment of the lyric. I was thirteen years old and if Mum and Dad disapproved of, "those long-haired creatures," that was all the reason I needed to love them.

The teenage defiance of fifty years ago returned as I shouted back the lyrics. Jagger was showing off all his legendary moves, running, shimmying, shaking and pointing as only he can. He didn't look or sound the slightest bit his seventy-four years. Mick Jagger, one of the greatest and most distinctive lead singers of all time, is miraculously still at the top of his game.

The Stones took us all the way back to 1966 with *Paint it Black*, the song that signalled the start of my black clothes only phase that so infuriated my mother.

The red lighting and enthusiastic woo woo of the crowd and we knew it was coming, the anti-establishment biggie, *Sympathy for the Devil.*

The crinkly faces couldn't lie with a giant video screen, reflecting every expression. They must have played those numbers a million times before but you'd never know it. Keith's characteristic gestures, the slight kick of the left leg, head thrown back and eyes closed in the moment. Ronnie Wood's rictus grin to the crowd was no pretence, and even the straight-faced Charlie Watts broke into a momentary smile now and then. The same commitment and attitude they'd had in the 1960s was still there. What the Rolling Stones represent is still meaningful to the eternal teenagers in us all, and always will be.

Florence returned for a triumphant duet with Mick on *Wild Horses* and an extended version of *Midnight Rambler* pleased the hardcore.

My only quibble, and it may just have been me, was with Keith's solo spot. I'm not a fan of Keith's high, thin, vocals but maybe the front man needed a loo break! Keith doesn't seem too bothered about disguising his thinning silver hair these days. The feathers and other pirate paraphernalia that he used to attach to his wayward locks has gone too. Only a colourful head band remained which, from a distance suggested a head injury. Pam Ayres would be pleased to know that Keef has looked after his teeth. They appear to be considerably younger than the rest of him.

The crowd went wild at *Brown Sugar* and when Mick shouted goodnight we knew it was only the beginning of the end. I'd been ticking off the items on my dream setlist and there was still a couple left to do.

The encore delivered the spine-tingling *Gimme Shelter* followed by the ultimate show closer, Satisfaction. Ours and theirs for sure. Next stop New York, for *Springsteen on Broadway*.

48

Boogaloo Down Broadway

In June 2018, Bruce Springsteen added *The Ghost of Tom Joad* to his Broadway show setlist, in protest at the inhumane treatment of migrants at the US border. This was the first song change in a hundred and forty-six performances and was warmly received by the audience.

I looked at my Twitter feed and learned that MSNBC newsreader, Rachel Maddow broke down on air as she described the forcible separation of babies and young children from their migrant parents at the US-Mexico border, and the use of so-called tender age shelters by officials of the Trump administration.

Making light of my own immigration experience in no way diminishes how I felt about this disgraceful treatment of families and children, and the subsequent inadequate statements by the Trump administration in the face of international condemnation.

'And what is your reason for visiting the United States?'

Welcome to immigration at Newark Liberty Airport. Obvious irony alert in the name but let that pass. After two merciless hours in a queue the question came as a blessed relief. It was the one I'd been waiting for.

'We've got tickets for *Springsteen on Broadway*,' I gushed.

'Nice,' he said, almost smiling, whilst flicking through the pages of my passport. He alighted on a page and looked up. Unsmiling.

'Whydya go to Iran?'

I blurted 'holiday' at the same time as Tim said 'business' and for one fleeting moment I pictured us being sent back on the next available flight. With the merest jerk of his head he told us we were off the hook, so we made a dash for the promised land of Manhattan before he changed his mind.

Months before, Bruce Springsteen had launched a unique theatrical project, designed to show us, his fans, what he described as his "magic trick." Namely, how his family background, life experiences (or lack of them) and some critical relationships had shaped his music and performing life. For Springsteen fans this was an irresistible proposition. It started with his memoir, *Born to Run*, which I'd already consumed and digested twice. Tramps like us just can't get enough of this stuff.

Negotiating the challenges that come with fame and fortune, whilst also sustaining a healthy and satisfying personal and creative life is Bruce Springsteen's speciality. In the music business that's not so much a magic trick, as a miracle. To hear the man himself reflect on his own story in intimate and frank terms was more than any fan could have hoped for. It was a gift.

I recall seeing a video of a different live show some years back, where a member of the invited audience was clearly heard saying, 'I love you Bruce.' The response from the stage was swift.

'But you don't know me.'

It struck me at the time that it must be difficult to deal with blind adoration from total strangers without losing some essential part of yourself along the way. It's happened to plenty. *Springsteen on Broadway* seemed to be the antidote to all that. On that stage, it was Bruce the man, puncturing his own Mr Born to Run /Mr Thunder Road image, and laughing at the guy who wrote those songs, the guy that couldn't drive a car at the time, and still lives ten minutes away from the town he grew up in.

Brilliant Disguise was one of two duets in the show that he sang with his wife, Patti Scialfa, and while it's essentially a song about revealing who we are to a partner, it could also stand for the relationship between fan and rock star.

It was Bruce the megastar that emerged from the stage door after the show to sign autographs, pose for photographs, and wave to fans on the street. As we waited, we had a glimpse into the finely tuned machine that kept the *Springsteen on Broadway* wheels turning, the assistants, the technicians, the security and the cars. By 10pm the drivers and minders were in position, headphones on, waiting for the call that said Bruce was leaving the building. Firm but friendly security staff chatted to us, whilst ensuring the traffic kept moving past and no one stepped out of their designated spot behind the barrier. We scanned their faces for clues as to when He would appear.

'He's the Boss. He decides. No guarantees.'

Ticket holders from other shows walked by, bemused. It was unbelievable that they didn't know who we were waiting for. Their reaction instantly upped the ante.

'No? You're kidding me! Springsteen comes out after the show? Really?'

At 10.40pm exactly, the stage door opened and Bruce, the icon, pen in hand, appeared ready and willing to sign books, albums, T-shirts and bare skin, if required. Plenty of lesser talents wouldn't bother but he was meticulous. I was just another crazy woman, the next one in line for a signature, thrusting a book in his direction. I wanted to say something meaningful but so did twenty or thirty others alongside me and we must have all sounded the same to him. I was overwhelmed and as he left his handwritten mark on my book I could only stammer pointless thanks and claw at the sleeve of his black leather jacket. As he turned to wave at the crowd I knew I would never forget this moment but he already had.

The next night was show night. Entering the Walter Kerr, is to be literally *in* the theatre as there is no foyer and no bad seat in the house. One look at the centre mic, the piano off to the side and you knew you wouldn't be straining to see the performer, that whatever this ticket cost, it was going to be worth it.

Theatre is about illusion, suspension of disbelief and pretence, but these things had no place in this presentation, though the standard conventions of theatre were observed.

There was a set of sorts, comprising a touring musician's gear stacked in front of a stark brick wall. The script, selected sections from the pages of his *Born to Run* memoir, interspersed, illustrated and accompanied by musical performance at the piano and at centre stage, on the guitar.

There were authentic characters, poetically and poignantly brought to life in the words and music. A red-faced father in a small town bar, a mother in high heels walking proudly back from work with her young son, a black saxophonist, the biggest man you've ever seen, honoured in time-honoured style at the piano in *10th Avenue Freeze Out*. Clarence, we learned, was waiting to be reunited with his bandleader in the next life.

There was drama and conflict in the telling and a tree bookending the performance, one that we know mattered very much to a young boy and the famous man he became. The show was memorably laugh out loud in places but mostly this was Bruce the man in confessional, reflective and serious mood. It was compelling and what he had to say about losing precious friends and family members was both profound and comforting.

I'd read these well-chosen words in the book and found them deeply affecting but having the author in front of you, telling you, with pain in his voice, of young men from his town that he knew and admired who didn't come back from Vietnam, was to absorb them for the first time. Then to witness *Born in the USA* as a howl of rage, a lament on lives lost and a country's shame was unforgettable. It was acoustic, but loud and raw, the sound hitting like punches to the head. It was the best version of the song I'd ever heard.

I've never been a fan of Patti Scialfa's solo voice, so when Bruce got to the part of the show where he recalled the moment he fell in love with her vocals, I really wanted to hear her sing the first line of *Tell Him,* rather than hear him describe it. A fleeting disappointment. I got over it.

Tougher than the Rest, sung by life partners, rather than new lovers, appeared to change its meaning. Not so much, I'm strong and can withstand all the difficulties we might face, but more, I'm a hard act to love in the long term. I'm the challenge. Bruce has written extensively about his battle with depression, which was hinted at in this show. This segment paid tribute to Patti's supportive role through the dark times.

The latter portion of the show moved away from the chronology of the personal to the political present. Trump was not mentioned by name but we all knew who he meant and we cheered the oblique spoken criticism and his comment on Martin Luther King Jnr's words, "The arc of the moral universe is long, but it bends towards justice."

'But I've lived long enough to know that arc doesn't bend on its own. It needs all of us leaning on it, nudging it in the right direction.' Bruce let *A Long Walk Home*, originally penned during the Bush administration do the talking.

It was this part of the show that came back to me most vividly the next evening. Walking back to our hotel we saw a crowd gathering on the pavement near Times Square. Three police officers were verbally abusing a black guy. They were still accusing him of resisting arrest even as they pinned his arms behind his back and pushed his face towards the pavement. The language was ugly and there were witnesses. No one said anything. America is a great country, but where was its conscience?

There's a moment in every Bruce Springsteen show that is transformative. Fans the world over saw that moment on the face of the guy featured in the *Dream Baby Dream* video. The one that the camera stayed on, as his lip quivered and his eyes filled. On Broadway, in New York, it came with *The Rising,* a hymn to the tragedy of 9/11. Prior to this moment I'd only seen this performed by the full band. As an acoustic solo with Bruce repeating the dream of life refrain like a ghostly echo, it was one of many emotional highlights.

Dancing in the Dark, as every fan knows, traditionally comes towards the end of the night, when Bruce pulls a lucky fan on stage to dance with the band. It's joyful and hopeful and in this show, it mirrored how tenderly he spoke of his elderly mother earlier in the evening, who despite dementia, hadn't lost her desire to dance.

I'd heard that Bruce recites the Lord's Prayer towards the end of the performance and I wasn't sure how I would relate to that, but in the context of his childhood home and the Catholic upbringing that enveloped him, it seemed natural. Whatever we believe, the words are buried deep within most of us, which is why a life-affirming departure from the well-worn phrases had such impact. 'Give us this day... just give us this day.'

The final song, *Born to Run,* and it had to be there, was a beautiful acoustic version, sung with maturity and gratitude. What a pity the call to respect the performer, and refrain from taking photographs until the curtain call was so spectacularly ignored. The majority of ticket-holders around us took out tablets and mobile phones to capture it from the very first notes. My other gripe was with those who couldn't sit for more than an hour without a bathroom break! So annoying in a small theatre.

In his summing up Bruce told us that in his life's work he hoped his, 'long and noisy prayer, his magic trick, would rock your very soul.' It did, and it still does. Long may it continue.

49

Don't Leave the Station!

Picture a train journey across Europe. What images come to mind? A seat in a claustrophobic old-style carriage with a collection of annoying strangers? Maybe an officious ticket inspector barking demands in a foreign language? Perhaps the situation prompts a general insecurity about negotiating the way to a new destination in an unfamiliar country? For me, all of these and more and I can pinpoint the source of my anxiety.

It was 1980 when we first saw *Caught on a Train,* a deeply unsettling television play by Stephen Poliakoff. The drama follows Peter, a British publisher during his eventful overnight rail journey from Ostend to Linz in Austria. Peter's comfort and peace of mind is repeatedly shattered by the accusations and demands of Frau Messner, an elderly Viennese woman sharing his carriage.

Hovering over this uncomfortable personal encounter is a wider sense of unease as Frau Messner contrives to make Peter leave the train on two occasions, against his better judgment. We learn that her relatives were members of the Nazi party and perhaps in an echo of that brutal time, the police board the train in the middle of the night, arrest Peter and take him away. He is only allowed back on the train when Frau Messner intervenes. By the end of the play she is cast in a more sympathetic light.

The anxiety prompted by the events depicted in *Caught on a Train*, had long been absorbed into our joint cultural consciousness. Thirty years later they resurfaced in Poland.

It was our second trip to the historic city of Kraków in the south of the country. The first time the weather had been wet and cold and we planned to come back in a different season.

This time the summer sun was shining. We re-visited the atmospheric old Jewish quarter of Kazimierz, retracing our steps to the nearby sites depicted in the film, *Schindler's List*, pondering on the terror that Nazi occupation once brought to the sunlit streets and squares filled with visitors. The area is young and vibrant with cool bars and cafés sitting cheek by jowl with evidence of the most terrible period in human history, including part of the original ghetto wall, built to separate Jewish citizens from the rest of the population, ahead of deportation to the notorious Auschwitz death camp, a few miles away.

The story of Oskar Schindler, the German entrepreneur that saved hundreds of Jewish lives through employment in his enamelware factory, was brought to the attention of the reading public in 1982 when Thomas Keneally's novel, *Schindler's Ark* won the Booker prize. It would be another eleven years before Steven Spielberg's film, *Schindler's List* brought the story to a wider global audience, delivering the predicted multiple, "Oscars for Oskar" at the Academy Awards in 1994. Less well-known is how Thomas Keneally came to write his book in the first place and why the journey from brilliant novel to lauded film took so long to complete. The fascinating answers to these questions can be found in Keneally's memoir, *Searching for Schindler,* my chosen reading material for this trip to Poland. As it transpired,

Keneally's book only came about through a chance encounter between the writer and an irrepressible shop owner in Beverly Hills. But for the purchase of a briefcase and the sheer persistence of Holocaust survivor, Leopold Poldek Pfefferberg, Keneally's book might have remained unwritten and perhaps Spielberg's film, unmade. Perhaps.

Our hotel was close to Kraków's main train station and a day trip beckoned. We chose the capital city of Warsaw. We were curious about the reconstruction of the historic centre after the war and the recommendation that this was the main attraction on a day trip to the capital.

The outward train journey took a good couple of hours. I'd slipped my paperback holiday book in my bag but didn't read much. I'm fairly sure it was a modern, high speed train.

First impressions of Warsaw after the beauty and atmosphere of Kraków were grey and dull. We took a meandering route towards the Old Town, stopping for a cold drink on a more colourful shopping street, showcasing young designers. Further along we encountered university students, demanding we take part in a survey, their abrupt English at odds with the request. An impromptu language lesson followed with me suggesting phrases like, "excuse me," and "please could I" would garner a better response from the British visitors. We parted, both sides laughing at my futile attempt to bridge the cultural gap.

The Old Town and the Market Square of Warsaw is a moving testament to resilience and the power of good to triumph over evil. In 1944, in an act of deliberate revenge against the Polish resistance fighters, the occupiers systematically destroyed Warsaw's historic centre in an attempt to obliterate centuries of

Polish history and culture. After the Second World War a five-year programme was started to rebuild what had been lost, to the exact and perfect specification of the original. The monumental undertaking was only completed in 1984. We spent the entire day meandering through the new/old streets and alleys, dipping in and out of museum buildings, admiring the spotless, colourful exteriors from a café table, and generally soaking up the atmosphere of what is now a UNESCO World Heritage Centre. In view of the history I found it depressing to see Nazi memorabilia for sale in antique shops on the side streets. I had seen similar in the flea markets of Budapest and Brussels and found it repulsive. There, as here, no one noticed as I quietly buried the enamelled swastika badges underneath piles of more benign objects before moving on.

Walking in the heat of the day had tired us out. We stopped for a reviving bite to eat, lingering a little too long. In the end, we made it back to the station for the return journey to Kraków with seconds to spare. A quick check for the right platform, and the anticipation of a relaxing couple of hours was ours as the train rumbled into view.

This was an older train with heavy, slam shut carriages and six-seater compartments with sliding doors. We scrambled into the last two vacant seats in the nearest carriage as the departure whistle sounded. Both window positions and the two seats opposite ours were occupied. Tim's rucksack went on the rack above our heads but I kept my bag on my lap. The train tickets and my book were in it and I would need those for the journey.

As the train pulled out I glanced at our travelling companions. I guessed they must all be Polish and I presumed they recognised we were not. We must have given off that visitor vibe by our demeanour, perhaps our clothing, and the subtle tension in the way we occupied the space. The two opposite us looked like a student couple. Their infrequent exchanges, indicated comfortable familiarity. She took out a magazine and he looked over my head, absorbed in his own thoughts. A glance to my left revealed a diminutive middle-aged man reading a newspaper. Polish headlines. Opposite, in the other window seat sat a taller individual, his head almost touching the rack above. He had a prominent forehead, little visible hair and a large oval face with deep set eyes. It was a balmy day and he was dressed for summer in shorts and a white singlet vest, revealing pale, hairless arms. It was the sort of attire you might wear for cycling and indeed he did have a bicycle, safely stored in another carriage, as I would find out later. Balanced on his lap was an incongruous brown leather briefcase, the sort that businessmen used to favour. The accessory was an eccentric finishing touch but more was to come.

We had been on the train for about twenty minutes when he unfastened the case, reached in and produced an egg. It was as if a Magritte painting had come to life. Piece by piece and with infinite patience, he removed the shell, depositing the bits in the briefcase before consuming the hard-boiled snack in dainty bites. He returned to the briefcase periodically, pulling from its depths, a couple of plastic containers containing more cold refreshments with a distinct odour. I was conscious of staring at Egg Man and that he might not appreciate being the entertainment. The book that had been in my lap, unopened since we sat down, became a handy diversion. The title and the front cover image were powerful, the content unmistakable. This was after all, a Polish story. I felt his eyes in my direction.

The journey continued for another hour. It was dark outside by this time and so I read on for a while until the rattle and movement of the train made me sleepy. I dozed off briefly but was roused by the sound of the compartment doors sliding open. Tickets were being produced for inspection. Ours were the last to be examined but something was wrong. A furrowed brow and a question, not directed at us but to the other travellers. The female student responded. I felt sick and even before she relayed the unwelcome news to us in perfect English, I knew what she was going to say. Our tickets said Kraków but the train was heading in a different direction.

We were racing through the Polish countryside with no clue as to where we were going. We'd been far too casual. I vaguely recalled seeing a K on the front of the train so hadn't given it a second thought. K for Kraków. Wrong. In this case K was for Katowice. Where?

The ticket collector went on his way and the rest of the carriage had a discussion in Polish, presumably about our situation. I started gathering our things. We would need to get off at the next stop. Not quite as simple as that. The student explained that we would have to stay on the train until it reached Katowice and then wait for another train to take us to Kraków. We were an hour and half away from Katowice at this point so it was surely a possibility that the last train back to Kraków would have departed from Katowice well before we arrived. I put this to the English speaking student and she in turn took soundings from the others.

Egg Man seemed the most knowledgeable on train times and took charge. He told us in fractured English, that unlike the others, he was staying on the train all the way to Katowice.

'You must wait long time for train to Kraków. I show you where,' he said. I could tell Tim was already calculating how best to use the waiting time. That this little error might give us the opportunity to experience a bar in another Polish city we hadn't yet seen.

'Any recommendations for where we could have a drink in Katowice?' he ventured.

Egg Man looked troubled and shook his head. 'Not go outside station. Not safe. Nowhere outside station. You stay in station.' It was an unambiguous instruction. The female student nodded in agreement and wished us a safe journey as she and her companion prepared to depart at the next stop.

The ice had been broken and Egg Man was going to save the day. Our eyes met and in that moment he tilted his chin at the forgotten book in my lap.

'Is Schindler story?' he said.

'Yes, but this is about the how the story eventually got made into the film, *Schindler's List*.' I held up the book so he could see the front cover and the prominent endorsement for the author by Steven Spielberg.

He half smiled in response. I wasn't sure he'd completely grasped what I'd said but I had misunderstood his reluctance to reply. He had something impressive to tell me and was just taking a moment to find the right words.

'I know this Spielberg,' he said at last. 'I am film director too. Spielberg know my film. He see my film. He like my film, and then make his film.' The tone of his response was a mixture of pride and gloom. Now he had our full attention.

What was *his* film? Was he telling us his work might have influenced Spielberg's? Galvanised the Hollywood director into finally getting around to making *Schindler's List* after the diversion of *Jurassic Park*?

Our questions were too complicated so we invited Egg Man, or to give him his proper title, respected Polish film director Leszek Wosiewicz, to print his name and the title of his film inside the front cover of my book. We intended to look for it on YouTube when we got home, as he advised.

His film, titled *Kornblumenblau* tells the story of a young musician who uses his talents to fight for dignity and survival within Auschwitz. It was released in 1989 and selected as the Polish entry for the Best Foreign Language Film at the 62nd second Academy Awards but was not accepted as a nominee. We knew little of this when we found ourselves on the platform at Katowice station, waiting for a famous Polish film director to retrieve his bicycle. He was good enough to find out where and when the train to Kraków would appear and with a final warning not to leave the station, as he was about to do, we said our farewells with grateful thanks.

It was a two-hour wait at the station for the train and we didn't move from the platform bench the entire time. Katowice station is something of an architectural marvel but we saw none of it. All our usual sense of adventure had completely evaporated.

The train eventually delivered us to Kraków in the early hours. We fell into bed and with the movement of the train still in our heads, slept like babies.

50

We Stayed at Home
23 March 2021

Today has been a declared a National Day of Remembrance, marking a year since we were first ordered to Stay at Home to Save Lives. A minute's silence at noon, and a doorstep candlelit vigil at 8pm to remember a year we won't easily be able to forget.

The UK has spent the majority of the last twelve months in lockdown, yet the shocking cost in human life is the highest in Europe with upwards of 126,000 deaths and counting, attributed to Covid-19.

This has been a year of enormous suffering and miraculous scientific and medical breakthroughs. Stories of separation, loss, grief, loneliness, hardship, unemployment, long-term sickness, mental health problems, poverty, impossible choices, and injustices are everywhere. The impact of never-ending restrictions plays out in public protest by some groups and a fear of freedom and what it might bring for others.

In a cruelly ironic twist, coronavirus, rather than Brexit, shows that limiting free movement doesn't stop the contagion from travelling where it will. We are being warned that a third wave of the disease affecting parts of Europe could arrive in the UK. This, even as our leaders are preparing to allow us to leave our homes and return to a fraction of the life we once led.

When previously liberty-loving politicians declare holidays and protests illegal at will, it's hard to see how freedom from the tyranny of a shape-shifting viral menace can ever end. The one bright spot on the horizon is protection through vaccination. Science has fought back and half the adult population of the UK has received at least one of the two required doses to prevent serious illness and hospitalisation from Covid-19. Meanwhile, EU countries are still grappling with multiple issues around vaccines, including distribution, trust in the safety and efficacy against new variants, and the challenge of rolling it out across a population.

It has been a year of living in the much reduced world of home and garden and understanding, as never before, how interconnected we all are, no matter the distance between us. As long as our nearest European neighbours battle with rising infections, crossing the Channel will be forbidden and travelling anywhere further afield, inconceivable. With Covid-19 and viruses like it predicted to stage regular comebacks, the idea that vaccine passports might be required for future entry to certain countries, and even concert venues is no longer fanciful.

I am weary of this dystopian life where reasonable expectations must be continually postponed. As if in defiance of it all, nature persists. Signs of spring, and lighter, longer days bring hope. In my dreams I dare to walk along a faraway shoreline, sing my heart out at a rock concert, people-watch from a bar in an unfamiliar city. Even hug my friends and family again. One day soon we'll begin to pick up the threads of the life we once had, knowing that we were the lucky ones. We survived a global pandemic.

51

Souvenirs

I'm a sucker for a travel souvenir. The bits and bobs that over the years have found their way into my suitcase for the return journey are part of me and my story. Not tacky, mass-produced objects, purchased for the sake of it but items specifically chosen to conjure the essence of a place once visited. Decorative, practical, indulgent and humble, these faithful reminders of places and encounters across the globe reside in every room of our home.

Some examples from a random kitchen shelf; hand-painted ceramics from a Tokyo department store; pretty food bowls, sold to us by a bemused restaurant owner in Hanoi; a rustic copper vase, purchased at a snooty house sale in Dubai. Inside a food cupboard, ten a penny in a Budapest market but culinary gold to me, is the little blue tin of superior sweet Hungarian paprika, complete with doll-sized wooden scoop and next to it, the last of three precious packets of rust red saffron from Iran.

I will admit to occasionally falling for something that seemed like a good idea at the time but out of context turns out to be faintly ridiculous. I once bought a complete *ao dai* outfit, including footwear, from Binh Tan market in Ho Chi Minh City. It was purchased to wear at my fiftieth birthday party celebrations that evening. The trying on, in a makeshift changing room, consisting of a length of material held in place by two giggling Vietnamese stallholders was a fun experience. Even with holiday sickness and the resulting weight loss, my *ao dai* felt a touch snug but I couldn't bring myself to disappoint such obliging sales assistants.

Back home, I ventured out in traditional Vietnamese dress only once, to a theatrical event. Matching fabric mules cut my feet to pieces and a small silk bag, a finishing accessory, fell to bits under the weight of a tissue and lipstick. Fully recovered from the stomach bug, the trouser fastenings felt uncomfortably tight and the tunic's elegant lines pulled in all the wrong directions. I should have donated the whole lot at the end of the trip instead of hauling it home. On the same holiday we bought a monochrome lacquered image, perfectly suited to life in our bathroom and a much better reminder of a beautiful country and its people.

That tour of Vietnam resonates in other ways. I only have to inhale the interior of another purchase, a hand-embroidered silk handbag, and I'm transported back to a Vietnamese market, via the pervading odour of fish sauce that lingers faintly in its fibres still, some sixteen years later. Now that's what I call a souvenir.

I learned everything I know about souvenirs from my mother and even inherited a few of her actual choices. Always the mistress of a great purchase in a foreign land, those small pieces of humble artisan pottery that she couldn't live without, from a market in Greece, a stallholder in France, now sit on my windowsills. Memories for sale. Summer sunshine captured for the dark days.

It was during summer 2019 that we'd put together an itinerary for a trip across the globe, designed to follow the sun whilst winter

2020 played out in the UK. From Dubai, we would fly to South Australia. There were friends to catch up with in Adelaide, and also Melbourne and Queensland. We intended to connect with Tim's cousin in Tasmania, a place we had never explored before. For the last leg of our trip, we planned to relax in Bali and Lombok, then a couple of nights in dazzling Singapore before flying back to the UK. As it panned out we arrived home little more than a week before full lockdown came into force in the UK. During that bleak time memories of our trip floated to the forefront of our minds like a series of gorgeous daydreams. As the weeks and months of restrictions continued I vowed I would never take the freedom to travel for granted. You really don't know what you've lost till it's gone.

So for the record, and in no particular order here are my mementos from that precious trip, not physical objects but fond remembrances of familiar places, and some striking new experiences.

Easily reached by taxi from Dubai, the Louvre Abu Dhabi opened with great fanfare shortly after we left the UAE and is the largest art museum on the Arabian peninsula. The exterior dome of overlapping latticework is designed to direct gentle rays of light into the cool white interior vestibule. Yet another architectural triumph for the region, although for me on this first visit, the curation of the permanent collection is what I took away.

The museum aims to show the history of human civilisation by placing art from diverse cultures and regions side by side, in a timeline that extends from the earliest settlements through to the present day. The approach makes for interesting juxtapositions of interpretations on a common theme from unconnected parts of the world, suggesting humankind is driven by the same creative impulse, whatever our differences. Inevitably, the curation has its critics and is more successful in the first few galleries where there is far less emphasis on Western art, although we found it ridiculous that the male genitalia on an Italian sculpture sported fake modesty leaves. Artistic expression can only go so far in the UAE.

No such limits at Hobart's Museum of Old and New Art (MONA), where thanks to its entrepreneurial owner, David Walsh, the exhibits, housed on three subterranean levels, are loudly and proudly visceral. Some are uncomfortably biological too, such as an ingenious, hands-on light installation in sync with the peculiarities of each viewer's heartbeat, and the infamous Cloaca machine. Suspended from the ceiling, Wim Delvoye's mechanical creation, built specifically for MONA, mimics the digestive process in continuous and realistic detail.

It's perhaps no coincidence that another of the Belgian artist's installations at MONA remains uppermost in my mind. This one, named Tim, is, at the time of writing, a living, breathing human, with an elaborate series of colourful tattoos on his back. These were completed by Delvoye some years ago and are pretty standard fare. A skull, a Madonna-like face, flowers, birds and fish. These adornments in and of themselves are not especially interesting but the human canvas on which they are etched is, in a number of ways. When Tim dies, as agreed by all parties, the skin on his back will be removed, preserved, framed, and delivered to the German art collector that purchased the work for thousands of euros. In the meantime, he has agreed to sit in galleries across the world, cross-legged on a plinth, lit to illuminate the artwork on his back. We came upon him in March, 2020. His residency at MONA began in November, 2019. He had been there every day the museum was open, silent and still, taking only fifteen-minute breaks every few hours. At the time I felt compelled to ask a gallery assistant about his mental and physical welfare. I found his presence and the story behind it strangely affecting. It was only later, after the museum had closed its doors to visitors because of the pandemic that I read about Tim, still in position every day, alone. Just like all the art at MONA he remained reliably in place, live streamed for online visitors, a testament to the enduring power of artistic expression as the rest of the world closed down.

Adelaide, in South Australia was our home for a while in the early 1980s. It will always be a place where I reconnect with my younger self, revisit the friends we made back then and indulge in a bit of nostalgia.

The colourful Central Market, always one of my favourite Adelaide institutions was still pleasingly hectic and diverse but far more gastro-orientated than circa 1982. I missed the fatty aroma of spit roasted "chooks" wafting through the air, as it did forty years ago. I even looked for the stand for old time's sake. Next generation artisan producers have moved in with an array of appetising ready-to-eat fresh foods, sandwiched between the glorious displays of fruit and vegetables. The market's upgrade mirrors the city's development as a whole and is a sign perhaps that tastes are now more sophisticated, pockets a little deeper.

We'd arrived in Adelaide just in time to catch the start of the Fringe. The popular accompaniment to the main Adelaide Festival features a huge programme of quirky outdoor performances staged in tents around the parkland, renamed *The Garden of Unearthly Delights* for the duration. As the evening crowds swelled to take in the more adult content, I was reminded of an installation I saw at the 1982 Adelaide Festival called *The Pavilion of Death, Dreams and Desire*. Back then, the joint project by the ceramic sculptor Mark Thompson and photographer Micky Allen became mired in controversy when the mildly disturbing visual content went on show in a rotunda in the park. Adelaide wasn't quite ready for it then, but in my twenties, I lapped it up. This time the exhibition that really stood out was *Yabarra: Dreaming in Light*. An Aboriginal story, thousands of years old triumphed as a walk-through presentation, using advanced digital projection technology to create magical special effects.

We were away for five weeks and during that time enjoyed food from multiple cultures and cuisines. What makes a meal a stand-out experience is so much more than the food on the plate. The company, the occasion, the level of comfort, the place, the service, time of day and general mood all contribute. When everything comes together and the food is great too, that's when the magic happens. *The Currant Shed*, just outside Adelaide in the McLaren Vale provided a wow factor lunch for our party of six. Between us we must have sampled the whole menu. A kitchen has to be supremely confident in the quality of the cooking to dispense with overblown descriptions, and instead create intrigue and excitement on how the different elements will all come together on the plate. I reproduce the menu here because the concepts were imaginative and original and each dish so well executed. It reads like poetry, an ode to deliciousness. Even classic combinations showed up as the absolute best versions of themselves. We couldn't move after this delicious feast.

Starters

Kingfish, chimichurri, sea grapes, sweet potato

Pork, peanut, chilli, bean sprouts

Zucchini, tomato, basil, olive

Melon, prosciutto, rocket, goat's cheese

Scallops, leek, pancetta

Mains

Beef, mango, chilli, bok choi

Eggplant, miso tofu, slaw

Chicken, apricot, coconut, almonds

Sardines, squid, chorizo, quinoa

Lamb, rhubarb, fennel, mint

Desserts

Chocolate, passion fruit, coconut

Peach, Thai basil, granola

Strawberry, milk tart, yoghurt, eucalyptus

Carob, citrus, hazelnut

Sea grapes, an element in one of the starters, are a type of textured seaweed, popular in Japanese cuisine. It was lunchtime, a warm day and some of our party were drivers so we mostly stuck to refreshing non-alcoholic cocktails.

The Indonesian islands of Bali and Lombok provided contrasting experiences. In the town of Ubud in Bali, where the predominant religion is Hindu, we dined on pork dishes, fragrant with galangal, lime and lemongrass. Our restaurant table offered stunning views across a valley of temples and palms and the evening air was sweet and warm, but for me this experience was outshone by a modest beach bar-cum-shack in Senggigi on Lombok island. With the unlikely name of *Nuf' Said,* the family-run enterprise served simply prepared seafood with two sambals – one spicy with chilli, the other green and fresh with coriander. With a view of the ocean, a cold beer to hand and skewers of freshly grilled prawns, it was lazy lunchtime perfection. We went back three times and on the last visit the owner proudly showed us the inflight magazine feature that must have brought a steady stream of visitors to his counter before Covid struck. I hope he's still in business. We should have found a great beef rendang in these parts too but the one example I tried didn't quite cut it.

On this trip, Tasmania came out tops for a local dish that surpassed all expectation. The famed scallop pie is a hefty number so requires a certain level of hunger to fully appreciate, but we were running out of time. It was our last morning in Hobart and the previous day we'd made a mental note to return to a fabulous looking bakery in Battery Point for breakfast. The displays of sweet and savoury pastries, pies, cakes and breads, plus a chalkboard of meal options for dining in, promised greatness. Unwittingly, we had stumbled on *Jackman & McRoss,* arguably the city's best known purveyors of a quality scallop pie.

It was nine o'clock in the morning and while croissants and eggs were what we wanted to eat, a scallop pie as a side order to try sort of made sense. Tim cut into the buttery puff pastry and a generous filling of scallops in a white wine and cream-rich sauce oozed out. There was a good balance of diced potato, carrot, onion and peas in the mix but the vegetables weren't doing the heavy lifting. The scallops, and plenty of them, were definitely the stars.

Everything came together in the seasoning and the subtle curry flavour in the sauce. Perfect fare if you happen to be hauling crates down on the docks and worthy of all the hype.

From a gourmet treat to a mass-produced Australian classic, with iconic status. Enter the Golden Gaytime ice cream. Our itinerary included a stay with friends in Maroochydore in Queensland. They'd introduced us to this sweet treat, as well the rain forest trail near Little Yabba Creek, and the pioneering zoo and conservation centre created by the late wildlife warrior, Steve Irwin. An ice cream on a stick, popular with kids and adults for decades is caramel and vanilla flavoured, dipped in chocolate and finished with a crunchy biscuit coating. Apart from the name, I could see the appeal. What's not to like?

Community dining on a large scale is a way of life in Singapore. The diverse choice of well-priced street food available at the popular outdoor hawker centres reflects the Malay, Chinese, Indian, and Indonesian resident populations. It's an informal, canteen-style experience and the food looked so good at the *ABC Brickworks* food centre that we were in danger of the place shutting up for the night before we made a decision on what to eat. We passed by row after row of tempting stalls, advertising spicy laksa soup, roasted pork, fried prawn noodles, braised duck, fish curry, and much more. Chicken Rice, a Singapore Chinese staple was what I was after. I watched the guy in charge at *Lian Xin Hainanese Chicken Rice* dispense plate after plate of beautifully arranged goodness from a tiny prep area before ordering. It was fascinating to see such skill on display at close hand. There was just about enough room for him, a rice cooker, a heat source and a pot of fragrant chicken stock. In less than a minute he'd carved and arranged chunky slices of juicy poached chicken breast over stock-soaked rice, added three punchy sauces on the side and cucumber slices for crunch. It was a perfect plate of food.

Any encounter with the animals unique to Australia is a thrilling experience. On an early evening stroll in the Adelaide Hills koalas nestling in the eucalyptus trees posed for our photos, their silhouettes standing out against a cloudless blue sky.

On another night in a Melbourne garden a bold pair of possums peered through the glass at the humans within. These were creatures that I had previously only been aware of as a pattering of feet across a roof and assumed they were fearful of humans. The garden lights revealed dirty grey coats, sharply pointed ears and spiteful expressions, so not at all the cute little furry creatures I imagined them to be. On the other hand, after a visit to the sanctuary and conservation centre at Cradle Mountain, I warmed to the notoriously fearsome Tasmanian devil. With powerful jaws that easily crunch through bone, stocky, strong bodies and a hideous vocal range, they have a reputation for aggression. Little pink ears suggested there was another more vulnerable side to these creatures. We learned that a contagious and debilitating facial cancer has caused devil numbers in the wild to dramatically decline. The disease affects the animal's ability to feed, so the poor things eventually die from starvation. Healthy devils at the sanctuary routinely scream and bare their teeth at feeding time as part of their carnivorous eating rituals. We watched a noisy young group at the centre who appeared to be biting and wrestling each other in anger, but like children were imitating adult devil behaviour in play. Better than being silenced by sickness or careless car drivers.

We stayed overnight at a nearby lodge in the Cradle Mountain National Park. A board indicated there were three walking trails, graded for length through the surrounding wilderness. We didn't choose the shortest route as we had plenty of time before dinner. The trail was signposted with the flimsiest of red ribbons, sometimes attached to trees or posts but inconsistently so. In one case a scrap of red material just poked out of the ground. In lots of places we just had to made a lucky guess and hope for the best. It was almost dark and quite cold when the lodge lights came into view. We passed a young couple just setting out on their walk, armed with torches and in high spirits. We didn't like to spoil their fun with fearful warnings but as we sat down to our meal, warm and safe we worried about them, still out there in the dark. Eventually, and with some relief we saw them come in for dinner and waved in recognition. Did they get lost? Yes, they said, laughing, that signage was useless, wasn't it?

In Tasmania for the first time, we explored the north eastern coastal town of Scamander and the surrounding area. Our generous hosts had loaned us their former family home with its idyllic lagoon views. Tasmania's renowned sites of natural beauty and historical significance were well within reach by car, including the spectacular Bay of Fires Conservation Area. The British navigator Captain Tobias Furneaux coined the name in 1773 when he saw the lights from Aboriginal fires along the coast. It is also the case that bright orange lichen covers the coastal rocks so the descriptive name is still appropriate, without the historical detail. Sites within this area are protected and are of particular cultural and sacred significance to the Tasmanian Aboriginal community.

We were looking forward to welcoming friends and family from Australia back to the UK during 2020 but of course it couldn't happen.

We booked our most recent trip during lockdown, in the hope that the advanced date would see travel restrictions lifted but with the niggling doubt that they might not. So we decided to play it safe and opted for a short stay in Tenby, South Wales. It was quite tame for us but in the teeth of wildly changing circumstances it felt daring to even think about packing our bags.

As the July date drew closer and the population was encouraged to holiday in the UK, if they must holiday at all, we should have anticipated how busy this popular tourist spot would be. We were just so happy to be going anywhere, it was a reality check to discover that Tenby's restaurants were not only booked solid for the week but were short-staffed to boot, thanks to the perfect storm created by Brexit and Covid.

A few eateries had dispensed with bookings altogether as unscrupulous visitors were exploiting the situation by making reservations at three or four places and then taking their pick on the night. *The Fat Seagull* café and restaurant had a no bookings policy for this reason and so after a lengthy wait in the pouring rain, we eventually bagged a table and some excellent food and wine on the first night. It wasn't our first choice but *Florentino's* already had a queue of hopeful diners waiting outside in case of no shows. Annoyingly, everyone seemed to be honouring their bookings at the most popular Italian in town. We asked if there was any chance of a dinner slot the following evening. The only time they could offer us was 4pm. We took it without hesitation. We would happily eat dinner in the afternoon, like toddlers and organise our day accordingly, a wood-fired pizza our reward for completing one leg of the Pembrokeshire coastal path walk from Tenby to Saundersfoot. A bus could deliver us back in time for our early meal.

The next day was brighter and so we took our time. A gentle walk into Tenby to enjoy the views over the harbour, the picturesque boats and coloured facades of the small hotels and cottages rising above the beach. After a coffee, onwards we went along a steeper rise towards the coastal path.

We had no inkling of how the day would end. That among the calls Tim would make, the one to the Italian restaurant to let them know we wouldn't make it was the one I would remember most clearly.

The truth is we were ill-prepared for what we were about to encounter. For this route we discovered, rather too late, was not a casual stroll through undulating landscape, although in some parts it was briefly that. For long stretches it was a treacherous hike through steep, muddy woodland, saturated from weeks of intermittent rain. I am not as sure-footed as Tim so my pace was painfully slow, even though there was the luxury of a handrail to begin with. A super-fit runner galloped past us, his feet bouncing off the surface of an impossibly steep incline. Our downward progress to the bottom of the slope was so slow he completed a circuit and overtook us a second time, great leaping strides propelling him uphill and away.

After what seemed like hours we reached the bottom and the path flattened out for a bit. A temporary respite. I generally enjoy walking but hiking is pretty much my idea of misery. I haven't been blessed with a great sense of balance. Or even an average one. I can't ride a bike or ice skate and I have never fancied skiing. I really wanted to appreciate the glorious views we were passing but instead I had to concentrate on my feet, where and how to place the next step to ensure I remained upright. It was exhausting. Like a tired child I kept asking Tim how far had we come, how much further did we have to go? The answers were always disappointing. As we climbed higher, edging along at a snail's pace, me constantly reaching for Tim's steadying hand, it was clear that the predicted two and a half hours to complete this walk in these conditions was hopelessly optimistic.

It had long ceased to be anything like an enjoyable experience but there was little point in turning back. Abandoning the path and retracing our steps would not have been any easier. Tim was trying his best to jolly me along when the path opened up and we found ourselves on the edge of a field. Views of Tenby harbour in the distance showed how far we had come.

We lingered there for a bit and Tim took some photos with his phone. There's one of me, my black raincoat flapping in the wind. I'm smiling and complete. When I looked at this image afterwards I saw a better version of me. A before photo. If only a comedy hand could have reached down from the clouds right then and plucked me away.

Further on there was a second scrubby field and beyond that, a caravan park. We struggled to find the right path at this point, unaware that there was a proper road, parallel to the caravan park which we could have taken. Hindsight, as they say is a wonderful thing but not by its nature, available when you need it.

Instead, we went in the opposite direction, across the damp grass, turning down towards what turned out to be the steepest and muddiest section yet.

This time Tim held my hand and we gingerly made our way down a set of uneven steps. I was weary now and grumpy. Time was getting on. At this rate there was a strong possibility that we would miss the bus back to Tenby. I kept thinking about that bus and what a blessed relief it would be when we were out of this situation, looking out, warm, dry and anticipating food. Meanwhile, we were a long way from those comforts.

Earlier on, in the trickier areas Tim had held on to me but he took bigger strides and I didn't enjoy the feeling of being dragged along. Anticipating the same, I pulled away thinking I'd be better following him at my own pace. We had only gone a couple of hundred yards when I slipped, instinctively put my left arm out to break my fall, and heard the terrible crack of breaking bone.

The swelling near the elbow started immediately. Tim kept saying everything would be all right, a reassurance to keep me calm but my logical mind was saying the opposite. I heard myself trying to work it out in breathless, panicky logic.

'I've done something terrible to myself, I heard a crack. How will we get out of here? No one will be able to find us.' There were no immediate answers and then everything went black. The next thing I remember was Tim leaning over me, saying my name. For a moment I didn't know why I was lying on the cold, muddy ground and then the pain set in.

Strange, and maybe it's only me but at moments of high emotion I immediately think of my parents, both deceased. What would they say if they could see me here, hurt and lying on the ground in the back of beyond? My mum and dad generally thought the great outdoors, and exercise in general was dangerous. A beach and a stroll along a busy promenade was as far as they ever went. For them, a walk along a remote coastal path was so far out of their experience they would have trouble understanding why anyone would put themselves in such obvious danger. Perhaps they had a point.

We were still debating what to do when three figures appeared from the opposite direction. A couple, and a boy of about seven or eight years walking between them. The adults, I assumed his parents, stopped to see if they could help. Amazingly, the woman was a nurse and confirmed by looking at the swelling and hearing the tale, that my arm was definitely broken but how badly she couldn't say. Tim decided to go back up the slope to the caravan park to get help. The coastguard could be alerted and there might even be a medic on site. It seemed a good plan and they offered to stay with me until he returned.

I watched Tim retracing the steps we had taken, hoping on my own behalf it wouldn't be a long wait, but also conscious that the youngster with them wouldn't want to hang around for long. I was sitting awkwardly on my raincoat, one arm protecting the other. The man had a bottle of water which he gave me, while the woman outlined the probable routine when I got to A&E. I tried to stay calm and attentive but I must have appeared distracted. The child was remarkable. He stood completely still, staring down at me with concern through large glasses. I felt so foolish, falling over and causing all this fuss when a child was out here, happily walking around without a problem. After about half an hour, though it seemed much longer, my mobile phone rang. Tim was on his way back. The coastguard had been alerted and an ambulance was on the way.

'You could go off now,' I said to the woman. 'I'll be fine, really. Tim will be back shortly and you've got him to consider.' I indicated the child who was still standing by his father. His position hadn't changed at all. He'd made no demands, hadn't spoken a word. It must have been at least forty-five minutes before we saw Tim making his way towards us and only then did the adults agree to go on their way.

In the hour or more that we waited for rescue only two more walkers passed us. They were an older couple, clinging to each other as they took baby steps forward. Together, and from my viewpoint on the ground they appeared like one enormous unstable creature with four legs. I held my breath as they came closer, terrified that one of them would lose their footing and their combined weight would fall on me. Tim gave them a warning to indicate my injury and made a sort of human shield until they made it past us.

Several more calls were made and received on Tim's phone before a burly coastguard finally appeared, mistakenly believing he would be dealing with a broken leg. The enormous first-aid bag he was carrying revealed nothing of practical help for a broken limb anyway, save for a blanket which on Tim's suggestion he put round my shoulders while we waited for the paramedics and the promised pain relief.

In a telephone conversation between the coastguard and the paramedics it was decided it would be too hazardous to carry me by stretcher to a waiting ambulance, but the alternative strategy sounded no less terrifying. They planned to carefully walk me back along the path we had come, up the muddy steps to the coastguard's vehicle. From there I would be driven to a parked ambulance waiting in the next field. Somehow it happened. I vaguely recall the strong hand of the paramedic to my right who had a firm grip on the waistband of my jeans from behind. The coastguard's arm was across my shoulders and I was instructed to inhale gas and air with each painfully slow step. Tim followed but not being able to see him behind us increased my anxiety. He said it took more than half an hour to walk about two hundred yards. I couldn't decide if the gas and air was actually taking the edge off the pain but it was a distraction. Once safely inside the ambulance, it was nearly another hour before we drew up outside A&E.

An angel in a green coat, splattered with plaster solution greeted me. The young guy from the plaster room had the kind of hair that grew around his head like a halo. With the light behind him, plus the effects of morphine, the illusion held and stopped me thinking about what he was doing to an arm that may or may not have been mine, as I floated above the bed.

He'd wisely spotted I still had my rings on and helped me to get them off my rapidly swelling fingers. I'd been more concerned that I was messing up the bed with my muddy boots but no one at A&E seemed at all concerned about this.

'Tell me where you were and what happened,' he said.

I would have this same conversation with different health professionals that day and the next but no one as kindly as this.

'I was walking on the coastal path and I just slipped. I put my hand out to soften the blow I suppose, and then I heard this awful crack.'

'That coastal path keeps me in work,' he said, nodding in grim sympathy.

The x-rays and a later scan revealed the damage, but it came disguised in medical terms that required translation. I still had a mobile phone and one functioning hand to google the initial diagnosis which read, "supracondylar fracture of the left distal humerus." Apparently, I had made a proper job of it and the bone had fractured in several pieces. Thereafter, the description included the word, "comminuted" to cover this. A plaster cast would keep everything stable until the surgeon reviewed the damage and made a decision on treatment. I was about to enter what would turn out to be a four-day residency in a Welsh hospital.

What with the number of emergency arrivals and Covid routines and restrictions, there was a long wait before I was taken to a ward. Tim wasn't allowed in and had to leave a bag of toiletries with A&E staff for delivery. I was still in an ante room when a healthcare worker placed the bag on my trolley, and it was dark outside before a cheerful porter finally came to collect me. It had been a long and traumatic day and I thought I would be able to sleep as the pain relief had started to take effect, but every time I closed my eyes the tape replayed and I was back on that path with the sound of breaking bone in my head. There was something else preventing me from peaceful sleep too. I was in bed but still wearing every item of filthy clothing, right down to my boots.

'Dey didn't do dat for you down dere?' said the nurse in charge, indicating my clothing and making a sucking noise through her teeth that sounded like extreme disapproval.

Despite my injury, and at my request, my soiled clothing was swiftly replaced with a clean hospital gown, the offending boots finally removed and a mound of grit and earth, brushed from the sheet. It made no sense to me that Covid mandated the daily cleaning of surfaces that nobody touched, but muddy deposits in a hospital bed could be overlooked. I was going to be a difficult patient but I'd be a clean one.

I wanted to open my eyes but couldn't summon the energy. Far off, I could make out sounds of activity, other patients murmuring, the hiss and ping of machinery. I became aware of a sequence of inflation and deflation coming from the wrappings around my legs, apparently there to prevent blood clots. With a supreme effort, borne of curiosity I prised my eyes open. I could just about focus but I didn't understand what I could see. I was staring at a plump, purplish shape, something like a small cow's udder with smaller puffy tubes half curled under it that were within my control to straighten. It was my left hand, at rest across my body, swollen and bruised from the twin trauma of injury and surgery.

A five-hour operation had begun promptly at 9am that morning. After three cancellations due to competing, more urgent cases I'd begun to think about coming back home to Essex for the surgery. When they came for me on the third day, I was just grateful that the decision had been made for me. There was hardly time to take in what was definitely going to happen before I was wheeled in to theatre. An apt description, for what takes place is high stakes drama, performed under bright lights by an ensemble cast of skilled technicians, each with their own assigned roles, all essential to the outcome. Masks and gowns for costumes, with the opening dialogue designed to reassure.

The star of the show, me, centre stage, mute, watched over by at least six pairs of attentive eyes. All this care and concern to piece me back together was overwhelming and I burst into tears. Someone called my name and that's the last thing I remember.

The action was necessarily brutal and bloody, the sounds, had I heard them, would have been excruciating. You have to be cruel to be kind after all. Much later I learned what is involved in performing a left distal humerus open reduction with olecranon osteotomy.

On that first afternoon, through bleary eyes, I became aware of a faint but disturbing trail of dried blood across the lower part of my left arm and the back of my hand It must have been left to continue on its way because a dark, sickly crust was still stubbornly visible around each fingernail.

Several weeks after the surgery we related the circumstances of the injury to two friends. We hadn't gone over it between ourselves, I guess because the aftermath of the operation and the practicalities around my recovery had taken over. Even though vivid flashbacks of the fall were all mine, I thought our recollections at the scene would be about the same.

'It was so kind of the couple to stay with me all that time while Tim went to get help,' I said. 'It was such a long wait, too, especially for a child.'

'What child?' said Tim.

'The child, with the couple. The boy. He was amazing. Didn't say a word all the time you were gone. Just stared at me. In a good way.'

'There wasn't a child with the couple. It was just them.'

'There was! A boy, with light hair and glasses, about eight years old. You must remember him?'

Tim laughed. Our friends looked bemused and at the same time, curious about my version. I seized on my chance to convince.

'He was there! I can picture him now. His glasses had black frames and he was wearing navy blue jogging bottoms.'

'Did you speak to him? Did he say anything?' said Tim.

'No, but I urged the couple not to stay with me after a bit because it wasn't fair to expect the boy to just stand there, waiting for you to come back. The couple wouldn't hear of going though, and the child didn't complain at all. Amazing.'

When pressed, I had to concede that neither of the adults acknowledged my concern about the boy and no direct conversation of any kind passed between them.

'They were just a young couple. There was no child with them. Really, there wasn't.'

The tiniest seed of doubt had been planted but it wouldn't take root. I know what I saw.

There *was* a child.

So, my most recently acquired souvenir, from Pembrokeshire, wasn't purchased and was far from welcome but it's a part of me now and will be my forever companion on all future travel adventures. A seven-inch scar, extending from the upper part of my left arm to just below my elbow. Under the skin a network of surgical metalware, a permanent reminder of a miserable walk in South Wales that, in spite of everything, could have been so much worse. If I had fallen on my back or my head this book would probably not have been finished.

Thank you to all the NHS staff that looked after me at Withybush General Hospital in Haverfordwest, especially Mr Dylan Jewell and the surgical team involved in the extensive repair work.

About the Author

Ruth Badley is mostly an author, ghost writer, enthusiastic diner, arts lover and dedicated Bruce Springsteen fan. Occasionally, she is also a freelance journalist and PR consultant for clients in the geospatial industry.

Back in 1981, she was an English and Drama teacher. A graduate of the Central School of Speech and Drama she left her first teaching post in North London to fly to South Australia to join her husband Tim, a land surveyor. While she taught at Adelaide's Adult Language and Migrant Education Centre, Tim's work with an oil exploration company was mainly in the South Australian bush. They returned to the UK in the mid-1980s with fond memories of Australia, New Zealand and the Far East. Ruth pursued a second career as a journalist, pouring her arts, travel and food knowledge into weekly newspaper features. Fast forward to 2015 and the two travellers, though considerably older in years remained eager for another big adventure which materialised into two and half years in Dubai.

It was in Dubai that Ruth developed the idea for her first book, the award-winning family memoir, *Where are the grown-ups?* The true story explores the impact of a whispered tragedy across three generations of the author's family.

Where are the grown-ups? has been widely praised by BBC radio presenters and featured in special interest newspaper and magazine articles. It was a recommended memoir on TV's Sky Arts Book Club, and a finalist in the memoir categories of the Independent Author Network Book of the Year Awards 2020, the Wishing Shelf Book Awards 2020 and the Page Turner Awards 2021.

Bite-sized World – a memoir of travel, food and live entertainment, is a collection of short stories, anecdotes and quirky observations, on the author's expat life in Dubai and trips to memorable destinations around the world.

Ruth Badley's books are available as paperbacks, ebooks and audiobooks on Amazon. Please leave a review or rating if you enjoy them.

To find out more about Ruth Badley's books or send her a message, follow her author page on Facebook:

https://www.facebook.com/wherearethegrownups

She can also be contacted via Twitter @RuthBadleyPR, on Instagram:@ruth.badley and through her website:

www.ruthbadley.com

Ruth Badley has two adult sons and lives in rural Essex with her husband Tim.

Printed in Great Britain
by Amazon